By Sue Harper and S. Lesley Buxton

TIME TO WONDER

A Kid's Guide to BC's Regional Museums

VOLUME 3: NORTHWESTERN BC, SQUAMISH-LILLOOET, SUNSHINE COAST, AND LOWER MAINLAND

RMB

TABLE OF CONTENTS

In memory of Mark Leslie Taylor who designed the first two volumes of this series. You are sorely missed.

LAND ACKNOWLEDGEMENT

We would like to acknowledge that when we visit, work, or research in the museums and centres in this book, we are working and exploring on the traditional and unceded territories of the following First Nations:

Coast Salish

Gidimt'en (Bear/Wolf) Clan of the Wet'suwet'en

Gitxsan People

Kwakwaka'wakw First Nations

Líl'wat7úl Nation

Nisga'a Nation

Nuu-chah-nulth First Nations

Nuxalk Nation

Salish Peoples, including the q̓icə̓y̓ (Katzie), q̓ʷa:n̓ƛ̓ən̓ (Kwantlen), and se'mya'me (Semiahmoo) Nations

səlilwətał (Tsleil-Waututh) Nation

shíshálh Nation

Sḵwx̱wú7mesh (Squamish) Nation

Stó:lō People including Leq'á:mel, Semá:th, Kwantlen, Sq'éwlets, Máthexwi, and Katzie First Nations

Tla'amin Nation

Tsawwassen Nation

Tsimshian First Nations

x̄á'isla (Haisla) Nation

xʷməθkʷəy̓əm (Musqueam) First Nation

We recognize these Nations have thousands of years of culture and history on this land, culture and history we value and hope to learn from.

MAP OF REGIONAL MUSEUMS

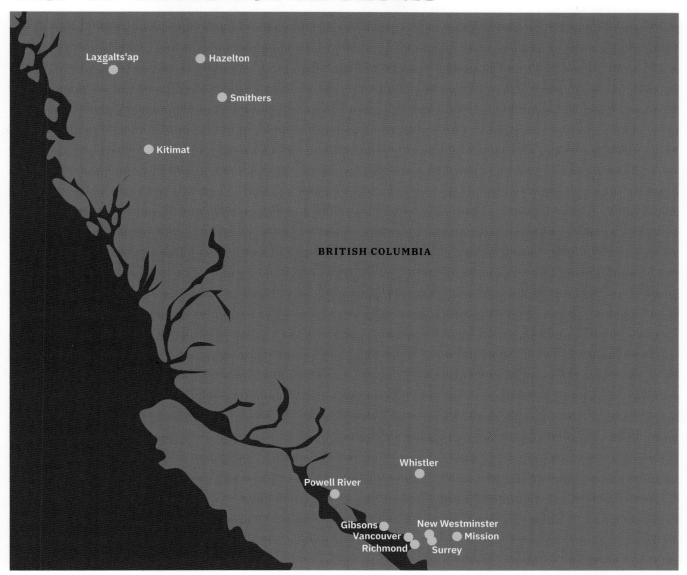

Laxgalts'ap

Hazelton

Smithers

Kitimat

BRITISH COLUMBIA

Whistler

Powell River

Gibsons

New Westminster

Vancouver

Mission

Richmond

Surrey

WHAT CAN WE LEARN FROM THE PAST?

Did you know two mind readers wrote this book? Yes, it's true, and we know exactly what you're thinking. You're thinking, *I'm a modern kid, what do a bunch of old things from the past have to teach me?*

Everything.

What? Everything?

Yes, everything!

What if we told you that when you enter a museum something mysterious happens. It's like being in one of those futuristic sci-fi movies where one moment you're in the present and then, suddenly, you press a button and *poof* you're in the future. It's like wearing a pair of X-ray glasses that gives you the power to see through objects into their past, present, and future all at once.

The objects in museums hold great power. Their stories come to life when you learn about them. A small, white desk may seem ordinary at first, but when you find out it once belonged to a famous writer, you begin to see the sparks. Add more details to the story, like, as a little girl of 6, the writer was forced by a **racist** wartime government to move with her family to an **internment camp** and leave school, and suddenly you see how people can survive all sorts of challenges. This is magic.

Sometimes objects invented in the past can teach us how to live better in the future. From **Indigenous** communities we have learned a great deal about the natural **resources** of British Columbia and how to live more **sustainably**. One example of this is the Musqueam and Stó:lō First Nations' fish drying rack that has been used for thousands of years.

This simple design harnessed the sun and wind to dry thousands of salmon filets at a time, providing food for the whole winter. Plus, salmon dried this way lasted longer than smoked salmon. This meant less waste. The very best part? This method of drying fish is still used today. This ancient design is the perfect example of how looking at the past can help us find inspiration. It uses both wind and solar power and teaches us how to create a balanced natural world.

When we visit belongings in a museum, it's like we are looking through a powerful magnifying glass that allows us to see the details of other people's worlds. We learn about their communities and what they value. It gives us perspective into other people's lives, which is a fancy way of saying it shows us what it's like to live in someone else's shoes.

Think about your belongings. What do you treasure most? What do you own that tells the story of who you are and who you might become? If we were to recreate your bedroom in a museum and look at your belongings, what would we discover?

Now you may be thinking, *what, hold on, I'm just an ordinary kid. Why would anyone care about me?* But history isn't only about important people like politicians, royalty, and inventors. It's about people like you, your best friend, and the two amazing writers of this book. Seriously, though, when you look at things like furniture, appliances, and tools owned by people in the past, you become linked to them. You also become connected by shared events and items.

Not long ago, our lives were completely changed by the

COVID-19 pandemic, and we were forced to quickly adapt. We wore facemasks, used hand sanitizer, and kept a metre away from our friends. It was a strange and lonely time. Did you know, over a century ago, something very similar happened? It was a worldwide pandemic called the Spanish flu. It was just at the end of the First World War and there was no vaccine. Like during COVID-19, a lot of people got very sick and millions died. People tried to ward off the illness with herbs, **camphor** amulets, red pepper sandwiches, and whiskey. They wore masks just like we did. This may seem like a very little thing, but knowing we share a similar experience with our **ancestors** helps us realize how much we have in common and how much the world has changed. It makes us empathetic time travellers who can learn from the past to make things better in the future.

NORTHWESTERN BC

Northwestern BC

BULKLEY VALLEY MUSEUM

JUST THE FACTS

WHERE IS IT? 1425 Main Street, Smithers, BC, V0J 2N0, in the historic Central Park Building
(250) 847-5322
bvmuseum.org/

Smithers and the Bulkley Valley Museum are located on the traditional, **unceded territory** of the Gidimt'en (Bear/Wolf) Clan of the Wet'suwet'en.

ARE PHOTOGRAPHS ALLOWED? Yes.

HOW DID IT START? Beginning in 1961, townspeople, including long-time resident Ernest Hann, gathered **artifacts** and **archives** representing Smithers and the Bulkley Valley. When the Smithers Centennial Library & Museum opened in November 1967, this collection formed the first public exhibits. The Bulkley Valley Historical & Museum Society was incorporated as a registered society in 1971.

WHERE HAS IT LIVED?

In 1974, when the collection outgrew the centennial library and museum building, the museum moved to the Central Park Building. This **heritage** building, built in 1925, was once the provincial government building and courthouse. The museum also stores collections offsite above the **municipal** hall and hosts events at the historic "Old Church" community events space.

WHERE DO THE ITEMS COME FROM?

Current and former residents have donated three-dimensional objects, documentary records, maps, and photographs since the museum was founded. The museum collects items that relate to the natural and human history of Smithers and the surrounding Bulkley Valley, including the communities of Witset, Telkwa, Houston, and Hazelton. In recent years, staff have begun collecting for the future by selecting items from recent history, including photos of Smithers during the first year of the COVID-19 pandemic.

HOW HAS IT CHANGED?

In 2016, the museum entered the digital world with the launch of its Collections Online website, https://search.bvmuseum. org. It provides free public access to the museum's entire collection, including over 2,400 artifacts digitized through photography, as well as thousands of digitized historic photographs, documents, newspapers, maps, and audio recordings that share the history of the region. The website is used by thousands of people each year, including researchers and students from Smithers and beyond.

discover how some everyday items were invented.

JOSEPH COYLE'S EGG CARTON

The egg carton was invented by Joseph Coyle in 1911.

Coyle was a newspaper publisher in the Bulkley Valley town of Aldermere, just east of Smithers. Aldermere is now a ghost town.

When Coyle overheard an argument between a hotel owner and a farmer about a delivery of broken eggs, he knew this was a common problem that needed a solution.

Coyle invented a lightweight cardboard package that would hold the eggs individually in slots, so they couldn't bang together. He began producing and selling the cartons through his newspaper business in 1915.

After Coyle moved his family and business to Smithers in August 1915, he became more serious about selling his egg cartons. One dozen handmade boxes sold for 35 cents in 1915.

Coyle **patented** the Egg Safety Carton in Canada in 1918, and the United States in 1927.

In 1919, Coyle moved to Vancouver. A year later, he invented a new machine, the Egg Carton Assembler, to **mass produce** his cartons. The assembler is in the collections of the Royal BC Museum in Victoria.

Coyle also invented a coin counter/separator, an automobile anti-theft club, and a pocket cigar cutter. He lived to be 100 years old.

JUST THE FACTS

> BULKLEY VALLEY MUSEUM

TAILOR'S SCISSORS

WHAT IS IT? This pair of metal scissors was designed for cutting fabric.

WHAT DOES IT LOOK LIKE? They are larger and heavier than kitchen scissors, or scissors for cutting paper. Tailor's scissors are designed to cut cleanly through thick or heavy-duty fabric without **fraying** the edges.

WHERE DOES IT COME FROM? In 2008, a descendent of the Aida family donated the scissors, as well as a tailor ruler, clothes hanger, and copies of family photos to the museum.

WHAT'S ITS STORY? Kintaro Aida used these scissors to cut fabric for suits and other types of clothing as part of his tailoring business. Kintaro's oldest son Tatsuo (also known as Tat) took over the business from his father and may also have used these scissors.

Tell Me More

It's not surprising that Kintaro Aida was a tailor. His father was a tailor in Japan. When Kintaro moved to Smithers, BC, he hired a local builder to build a **rooming house**, tailor shop, and laundry just off the town's main street. The family lived in the house next door. Kintaro ran the tailor shop and the rooming house, and his wife Sadako ran the laundry. The business was open for 29 years, closing in 1951.

Bulkley Valley Museum
(jpg 2015.13.2)

Bulkley Valley Museum (P6732)

WOULD YOU BELIEVE?

Fujio, the second-oldest Aida son, was a champion ski jumper. In 1939, he won the Class B ski jumping event at the BC Ski Championship in Wells, BC. According to the local newspaper, Smithers athletes Fujio Aida, Chris Dahlie, and Graham Collison won more awards than athletes from any other BC town or city that year.

My Turn

Scissors have many different uses. For example, the scissors Mr. Aida used were for tailoring. How many different types of scissors can you think of? Consider the house, the garden, businesses, and hospitals. Ask an adult to add to your list.

CONNECTIONS

These scissors represent the history of the Aida family, but there were other Asian Canadians who helped build Smithers from its earliest days. Japanese Canadians, including the Katsuros, George Ichikawa, and the Fushimis, as well as Chinese Canadians like Smithers' Bakery owner Mah Yoke Tong, ran businesses, raised families, and contributed to the growth and development of the town.

Bulkley Valley Museum (P6769)

WHY IS THE PAIR OF SCISSORS IMPORTANT IN THIS AREA?

Kintaro and Sadako Aida immigrated to Canada from Japan. Their five children, Tatsuo, Fujio, Tetsuo, Asao, and Sumiko, were born in British Columbia. The Aidas, especially their sons Tatsuo, Tetsuo, and Fujio, were very involved in the Smithers community. They played sports, supported local causes, and served on social committees.

During the Second World War, thousands of Japanese Canadians in BC were forced into internment camps. The town of Smithers fell outside the "protected zone," so the Aidas were not sent to the camps. They did, however, face **racism** in their community. Some people believed they were spies. Others threatened that they would be forced to leave Canada after the war. This pair of scissors reminds us not only of the Aida family's contributions to the community but also of the resilience of Japanese Canadians during this dark **period** of history.

JUST THE FACTS

PLANE PROPELLER BLADE

WHAT IS IT? This propeller blade came from a US Air Force B-36 bomber that crashed in the mountains near Smithers.

WHAT DOES IT LOOK LIKE? Think of a ceiling fan with really long blades. This blade is 183 centimetres long, the height of an average door. It bent in the middle when it hit the ground.

WHERE DOES IT COME FROM? Someone took the propeller from the crash site. That same person or someone else dropped it off at the Terrace airport in the middle of the night for the cadets. It was eventually donated to the museum.

WHAT'S ITS STORY? The United States Air Force used this plane in the 1950s during the Cold War.

Tell Me More

The B-36 bomber had six engines, each powered by a propeller with three blades. The plane's engines and propellers were behind the wings, which pushed the plane forward. This design used less fuel so the plane could fly longer missions without having to stop for refuelling.

My Turn

Nuclear technology can be used to create bombs, but doctors can also use it to help understand our bodies much better. With the help of an adult, find out some ways doctors use nuclear technology to help us.

CONNECTIONS

In the history of the US Air Force, the crash of Bomber 075 was the first (but not last) accident involving a nuclear weapon. "Broken Arrow" was a code name given for these kinds of accidents. This piece of Cold War history reminds us how close the world came to a third and deadly nuclear war throughout much of the mid-20th century.

WHY IS THE PLANE PROPELLOR BLADE IMPORTANT IN THIS AREA?

Between 1946 and 1991, the United States and the **Soviet Union** were involved in a power struggle. One way the countries showed their strength was by building powerful nuclear bombs.

On February 13, 1950, Bomber 075 was flying from Alaska to Texas, carrying a Mark IV "Fat Man" atomic bomb. Its mission was to **simulate** the conditions of a US attack on the Soviet Union. It was so cold the propellors iced up, and engines 1, 2, and 5 caught fire. The captain was ordered to detonate the bomb over the ocean and set the automatic pilot so the plane would crash into the water. The crew dropped the bomb and then parachuted out, but instead of crashing into the ocean, the plane ended up crashing about 300 kilometres inland on Mount Kologet, around 166 kilometres north of Smithers. How the plane got there is one of many mysteries surrounding the crash.

Northwestern BC

KSAN HISTORICAL VILLAGE AND MUSEUM

JUST THE FACTS

WHERE IS IT? 1500 Highway 62, Hazelton, BC, V0J 1Y0
(250) 842-5544
www.ksanvillage.ca/

Home of the Gitxsan People for over 8,000 years.

ARE PHOTOGRAPHS ALLOWED? Only outside. No photos are allowed in the museum or inside the Longhouses.

HOW DID IT START? Before the historical village was constructed, in 1959 the Skeena Treasure House Association opened a museum on the banks of the Skeena River in Old Hazelton, where it housed a collection of treasures belonging to the Peoples of the Upper Skeena.

Images courtesy Ksan Historical Village and Museum.

WHERE HAS IT LIVED?

As the collection grew, the association decided to create a historical village with traditional Gitxsan Longhouses. Ksan Historical Village and Museum opened on August 12, 1970.

WHERE DO THE ITEMS COME FROM?

Most of the items have been donated by individuals. Some are on loan from other museums.

HOW HAS IT CHANGED?

Wilp Gisk'aast (Fireweed House), which is also the treasure house, is the original museum building that was moved from Old Hazelton to the new site. The museum and gift shop; a wood-carving workshop, where you can see a carver at work; a silkscreen studio; and three additional Longhouses complete the village. Eagle House is also a restaurant.

In a museum you can:

learn about Indigenous regalia and how it is used in ceremonies.

HAXSGWIIKWS (WHISTLE)

Images courtesy Ksan Historical Village and Museum.

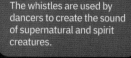

The whistles were carved from cedar and possibly birch.

The whistles are used by dancers to create the sound of supernatural and spirit creatures.

Dancers use whistles during ceremonial dances.

Sometimes dancers hide whistles in their costumes, so the sound is a surprise to the audience.

Different-sized whistles are used for different ceremonies. Each size makes a different tone and sound.

Whistles are also used to call on the spirits.

Some whistles play only a single note, while others can play two or three notes. Can you tell from the pictures which play multiple notes?

When whistles are used during songs and dances, they add to the emotion in the room.

HOOBIXIM HASG̱ALTX̱W MATX̱ (GOAT HORN SPOON)

JUST THE FACTS

WHAT IS IT? This spoon is like one you might use as a serving spoon, but it is made from a goat's horn.

WHAT DOES IT LOOK LIKE? Each spoon looks slightly different. Generally, the bowls of the spoons are shallow and long. Sometimes the handles are carved with a design.

WHERE DOES IT COME FROM? All the spoons were donated by local people.

WHAT'S ITS STORY? Families would use these spoons for serving and for eating. They were used in daily life, as well as for ceremonial feasts.

Tell Me More

To create a goat horn spoon, artists boil the horn until the outside is flexible and the boney part in the middle can be popped out. They then make a cut down the middle of the horn and bend it into a shape similar to the spoon they want to create. When the horn is dry, it is cut into its final shape and polished to a smooth, shiny finish. At this point, the artist may decide to carve the handle.

Image courtesy Ksan Historical Village and Museum.

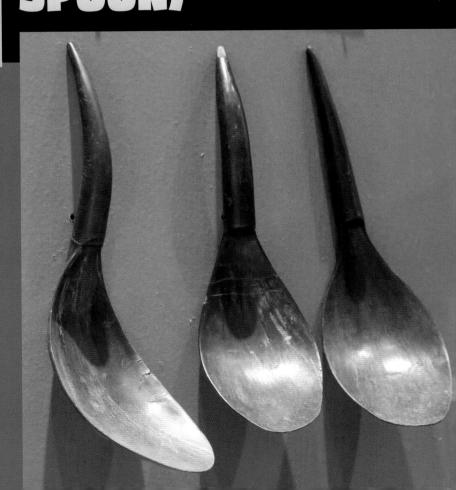

WOULD YOU BELIEVE?

The outer layer of a goat's horn is made from keratin, the same material that makes our nails and hair and horses' hooves. It doesn't stain, so these horn spoons are perfect for serving and eating food that stains like blueberries.

My Turn

Goat horn spoons are both practical and beautiful works of art. What other objects can you think of that are both useful and beautiful?

The art of carving goat horn spoons is in danger of disappearing. In Alaska, Steve Brown, a master carver, has been teaching a new generation of Indigenous artists how to create these spoons, keeping the tradition alive.

Image courtesy Ksan Historical Village and Museum.

WHY IS THE GOAT HORN SPOON IMPORTANT IN THIS AREA?

Mountain goats were usually hunted in summer or fall. After a kill, the Gitxsan People made a tobacco offering to thank the animal for giving up its life. As well as the horns, almost every other part of the animal was used – the hide for clothing or bedding, the wool for weaving, and the meat for eating. As you can see, mountain goats played an important part in village life.

Goat horn spoons were also used for trading with other Nations. Oolichan oil is not available in the Upper Skeena area. This oil kept very well, was a source of energy, and was also used in healing. The Gitxsan People would trade objects, including goat horn spoons, for this important fish oil.

JUST THE FACTS

› KSAN HISTORICAL VILLAGE AND MUSEUM

WILP LAX GIBUU (WOLF HOUSE)

WHAT IS IT? This building is a reconstruction of a Longhouse belonging to the Wolf Clan.

WHAT DOES IT LOOK LIKE? While it is smaller than a traditional Longhouse, it has the same features – an earthen floor, a firepit in the middle, a house pole, and tiered seating and living areas. There is also a trap door at the back of the house.

WHERE DOES IT COME FROM? Wilp Lax Gibuu was built as part of the historical village.

WHAT'S ITS STORY? The Longhouse would traditionally have been home to members of one Clan. During the winter months, families within the same Clan would live together.

Image courtesy Ksan Historical Village and Museum.

Tell Me More

To enter the Longhouses, visitors must take a tour led by a person knowledgeable about Gitxsan culture. The doorway to Wolf House is unlike any of the others in the village. You walk through the bottom of a Totem Pole! Only one adult can fit through the door at one time. If enemies tried to get through the entrance with their weapons and helmets, they would have a very hard time. This would give those in the house time to go through the trap door and hide in the room under the house. The Chief always slept at the back of the house, where he had a view of the front door.

WOULD YOU BELIEVE?

The Gitxsan People built tunnels leading from the room underneath the Longhouse away from the village and into the forest. If the village was raided by another Nation, the families would use the tunnel as an escape route.

My Turn

Do you have any traditions that have been passed down from older generations? How have they been taught to you?

 CONNECTIONS

Feasts are one way to pass the wisdom of the past to the next generation. While taking part in feasts, young people learn about governance, correct behaviour, and rules. The feast hall is also where houses and Clans make important decisions about governing.

WHY IS THE WILP LAX GIBUU IMPORTANT IN THIS AREA?

Today, items in Wolf House – also known as the feast house – help visitors learn about *yukx,* or feasts, that are an essential part of Gitxsan culture. Feasts are held for many reasons. For example, death feasts are held to settle the deceased person's debts and acknowledge people who have helped the person during their lives. Feasts are also held for Totem raising, unveiling new masks, and naming children. The Chief who holds the feast gives gifts to each invited guest. Stories are told through songs and dances with wonderful costumes and masks. And, of course, there is food. Lots of food. The young people of the hosting Clan are usually the servers, and the host family always eats last. In 1884, the Canadian government banned the feast system, but feasts were so important to the Gitxsan way of life, the people held them in secret until 1951, when the law was dropped.

KITIMAT MUSEUM & ARCHIVES

JUST THE FACTS

WHERE IS IT? 293 City Centre, Kitimat, BC, V8C 1T6
(250) 632-8950
www.kitimatmuseum.ca
Kitimat Museum & Archives is located on the traditional and unceded territory of the x̄á'isla Nation.

ARE PHOTOGRAPHS ALLOWED? Yes.

HOW DID IT START? To celebrate Canada's 100th birthday, the governments of Canada and British Columbia provided money to cities and towns for centennial projects. Many Canadian museums started in this way, including Kitimat Museum & Archives. There were many different ideas submitted to the Kitimat Centennial Project Committee, but the committee chose the museum project. Four years later, in 1969, the museum opened.

WHERE HAS IT LIVED?

The museum still lives in the same location.

WHERE DO THE ITEMS COME FROM?

The Kitimat Centennial Project Committee donated the very first item, a 1.2-metre family pole carved by x̄á'isla (Haisla) artist Sammy Robinson. Most objects come from donations, but once in a while the museum will purchase an item for the collection.

HOW HAS IT CHANGED?

The museum is still in its original home, but there have been many changes to what's inside. Naturally, the permanent collection that tells the stories of the x̄á'isla First Nation, the early **settlers**, the Kenney Dam Power Project, and area geology and wildlife has grown. Visitors can also learn from **temporary exhibits** that change throughout the year. Finally, the museum was built on two floors and wasn't always **accessible** to everyone. Because an elevator was added, everyone can now see the exciting treasures the museum has to offer wherever they are displayed.

Images courtesy Kitimat Museum & Archives.

In a museum you can:

learn about Indigenous regalia worn during ceremonies.

'ÍKSDUQ^WIA (EAGLE) FRONTLET

Museum photos of 'íksduq^wia (Eagle) frontlet with permission from artist Lyle Wilson.

The x̱á'isla (Haisla) 'íksduq^wia (Eagle) frontlet is part of a headdress worn by a Chief or other high-ranking person during ceremonies.

It was created by artist Lyle Wilson.

Lyle says, "The frontlet has an interesting mix of material: the fastening chinstrap is really old-fashioned cotton string from my grandfather's commercial fishing days; the cedar bark 'basket' was done by a Haida-Kwakwa̱ka̱'wakw-Irish weaver; the **baleen** rim I traded from Bella Bella; bottom buttons and leather came in trade from a Jewish fisher/teacher/machinist friend; the top buttons purchased from someone that came back from Thailand; and the ermine from a Vancouver fur company."

The materials used on a frontlet represent the wealth and power of the person who wears it.

Lyle grew up in the Haisla tradition of hunting, fishing, and gathering, and then attended university and art school. He is always learning about Haisla art through research and through his own painting and carving.

Although Lyle was born into the Beaver Clan (his mother's), he was formally adopted into his father's Clan, the Eagle Clan. He carved his Clan's crest on this frontlet.

Lyle donated the frontlet to the museum in 2021, just one of many art pieces he has donated to provide a **legacy** of his artwork for the communities of Kitamaat Village and Kitimat.

JUST THE FACTS

WHAT IS IT? This pin celebrates the naming of the Kenney Dam, named after Edward T. Kenney, Liberal Minister of the Department of Lands and Forests for British Columbia from 1933 to 1953.

WHAT DOES IT LOOK LIKE? The pin is round, with a shiny silver colour. Written in capital letters in three lines across the surface reads, "KENNEY DAM, ALCAN, MAY 10, 1952."

WHERE DOES IT COME FROM? Mrs. D.L. Norrington of Summerland, BC, donated it in 1983, in memory of her husband, Judge C. James Norrington.

WHAT'S ITS STORY? This pin was given to people who attended the naming of the Kenney Dam, part of the Aluminum Company of Canada (Alcan) project in northern British Columbia.

› KITIMAT MUSEUM & ARCHIVES

KENNEY DAM SOUVENIR PIN

Tell Me More

Smelting aluminum takes a huge amount of energy. Alcan built the Kenney Dam to generate hydroelectricity for its smelters. The dam is just under 100 metres tall, almost as tall as a soccer field is long. It is made from millions of cubic metres of rock, gravel, and clay. To create the reservoir that sits behind the dam, the company reversed the natural eastward flow of the Nechako River to make it flow westward into a chain of lakes. Water from the reservoir flows through a 16-kilometre tunnel that drops almost 800 metres (about 530 refrigerators piled on top of each other) before it arrives at the powerhouse.

WOULD YOU BELIEVE?

Bauxite is used to make aluminum, but Canada does not have any bauxite mines. All the raw material is brought in from other countries like Australia. Most of Canada's aluminum products go to the United States.

My Turn

How many products can you think of that use aluminum? How would your life be different without aluminum?

CONNECTIONS

Many things have changed since the 1950s. In 1993, the Cheslatta sued the Canadian government over their loss of land and settled for about seven million dollars. In 2019, the BC government signed an agreement with the Cheslatta People for financial and land compensation. Rio Tinto, the current owner of the aluminum smelters at Kitimat, has replaced the old smelters with new, more environmentally friendly models. In 2020, it signed the New Day Agreement with the Cheslatta Carrier Nation that promises the Nation training, employment, business opportunities, and **environmental stewardship** of the Nechako **Watershed**. The New Day Agreement also provides scholarships for Cheslatta students through the New Day Scholarship Fund.

WHY IS THE KENNEY DAM SOUVENIR PIN IMPORTANT IN THIS AREA?

The Alcan project provided many jobs to workers from around the world and created an aluminum smelting industry in western Canada. There was celebration when the dam was named, with people receiving these pins as souvenirs. But the dam also has a sad history. The Cheslatta T'En, members of the Carrier First Nation, had lived in the Nechako River Valley for more than 10,000 years. This is the valley that was flooded for the reservoir. Non-Indigenous ranchers in the same valley were told two years before they had to leave their properties and were offered $1,544 per hectare for their land. The Cheslatta were told fewer than two weeks before they had to leave their homes and were offered $77.22 per hectare for their land. If they didn't agree to sign over their property, they were not offered anything. Their villages (including graveyards), pastures, and the land where they hunted were submerged under the reservoir water.

JUST THE FACTS

WHAT IS IT? This pole was carved by Sammy Robinson, Chief Jasee, Hereditary Chief of the Beaver Clan and highest-ranking Chief of the x̄á'isla (Haisla) Nation.

WHAT DOES IT LOOK LIKE? Unlike many poles you may have seen in books or real life, this is a small pole, 125.7 centimetres tall. It is made from yellow cedar.

WHERE DOES IT COME FROM? The Kitimat Centennial Committee presented the pole to the museum.

WHAT'S ITS STORY? In 1967, Canada celebrated its 100th birthday by hosting an international exhibition called Expo 67. The exhibits in the "Indians of Canada" pavilion told Canada's history from an Indigenous point of view. Sammy Robinson completed this pole at that exhibition.

Tell Me More

The pole features x̄á'isla Clans, Eagle, Beaver, Blackfish (Killer Whale), Salmon, and Raven. At the base of the pole is Beaver (Sammy's Clan). Behind Beaver is Grizzly with Salmon, the crest of Sammy's wife, Rose. Above is the legendary figure Tah-nees, a wild man from a high family. Frog, the figure above Tah-nees, is from a Clan that was wiped out during a flu pandemic in 1918. Then there is Wee-git (Raven), who can turn himself into any other creature. He has Salmon in his beak. Owl sits above Wee-git. The next figures are Killer Whale with a woman clinging to its back. Eagle sits on the top of the pole.

Northwestern BC
› KITIMAT MUSEUM & ARCHIVES

YELLOW CEDAR X̄Á'ISLA FAMILY POLE

Image courtesy Kitimat Museum & Archives.

WOULD YOU BELIEVE?

Tah-nees, one of the pole's figures, appears at ceremonies to honour others of high rank by biting them!

My Turn

Why do you think art is so important to a culture?

CONNECTIONS

The figures on the pole tell important stories. The woman on the back of the whale is the wife of Sa-ga-dee-law. She was standing in the shallow sea water on a beach, washing her robe – a rare albino sea otter skin – when Killer Whale captured her. Sa-ga-dee-law, with several other men, paddled his canoe to the place in the sea where the whale dove down. To save his wife, Sa-ga-dee-law made a long pole by tying five cottonwood poles together and sinking one end to the bottom of the sea. He then climbed down the pole into the underwater world where he found a world similar to his own. After many adventures, he recaptured his wife and returned home with her.

WHY IS THE YELLOW CEDAR FAMILY POLE IMPORTANT IN THIS AREA?

This pole was the very first object given to the museum. It is one of many pieces that introduce visitors to the arts and culture of the x̄á'isla. For over 9,000 years the x̄á'isla – who are made up of two historic bands, the Kitamaat and Kitlope – have lived in this area. Today, x̄á'isla artists continue to learn and practise the traditional skills of carving, painting, and weaving. But, like all artists, they bring their own interpretations to their craft. You may have already read about Lyle Wilson's carving of the Chief's frontlet. Lyle says he was most influenced by his Uncle Sammy – yes, the same one who carved this pole! When you visit the museum, you can see how Clara Bolton and Ella Grant have used traditional weaving methods to create beautiful modern baskets. The carvings, weavings, and paintings show how x̄á'isla culture continues to thrive.

HLI G̲OOTHL WILP-ADOK̲SHL NISG̲A'A (NISG̲A'A MUSEUM)

JUST THE FACTS

WHERE IS IT? 810 Highway Drive, Lax̱galts'ap, BC, V0J 1X0
(250) 633-3050
nisgaamuseum.ca/
Hli G̲oothl Wilp-Adok̲shl Nisg̲a'a (Nisg̲a'a Museum) is located on Nisg̲a'a lands in the traditional village of Lax̱galts'ap.

ARE PHOTOGRAPHS ALLOWED? Yes, for personal use, but flash is not permitted.

HOW DID IT START? The museum opened on May 11, 2011. It honours the history of the Nisg̲a'a People who have lived along the K̲'alii-Aksim-Lisims (Nass) River in northwestern BC since **time immemorial**. In 2000, the **Nisg̲a'a Final Agreement** came into effect with the governments of BC and Canada. The treaty included **repatriation** of over 300 cultural items wrongfully taken from the Nass Valley. These belongings are now in the museum.

Images by Gary Fiegehen, courtesy Nisg̲a'a Lisims Government.

WHERE HAS IT LIVED?

The museum was built in the village of Lax̱galts'ap to receive belongings that were taken when the government of Canada and Christian missionaries prevented Indigenous Peoples from practising their ceremonies and traditions. Families' belongings were stolen or traded, or sold for far less than their worth. These possessions were welcomed home from the Canadian Museum of History, Royal BC Museum, and Anglican Church.

WHERE DO THE ITEMS COME FROM?

These items are personal and ceremonial belongings of people who lived in the Nass Valley. Many of them were passed down through **hereditary lineages** and show family relationships. **Performative masks**, **spiritual** charms, rattles, puppets, and other ceremonial **regalia**, including headdresses, Raven rattles, blankets, and bentwood boxes, belonged to spiritual leaders, dancing society members, Chiefs, and **Matriarchs**.

HOW HAS IT CHANGED?

Repatriation of belongings from museums is ongoing worldwide. In 2023, the Wilps Ni'isjoohl memorial *pts'aan* (Totem Pole) was returned from the National Museums Scotland. The cultural treasures Elders and community members choose to bring back focus on Nisg̲a'a spirituality and spiritual practices in daily life, including those of traditional healers. The museum honours the past through the Anhooya'ahl Ẃahlingigat (Ancestors' Collection). In the museum, Nisg̲a'a People can access their cultural heritage and reaffirm or learn traditional values and spirituality. Experiences at the Nisg̲a'a Museum are guided. Information is shared in a traditional way through storytelling. Youth and young adults from surrounding communities feel pride in their identity as they teach Nisg̲a'a history and heritage to visitors.

In a museum you can:

learn the histories of the land and of Indigenous Peoples as they are told through their stories.

MASK OF GWAAX̱TS'AGAT

Images by Gary Fiegehen, courtesy Nisg̱a'a Lisims Government.

This mask represents the *naxnok* (supernatural being) Gwaax̱ts'agat. It was carved over 100 years ago.

The Tseax volcano cone erupted over 250 years ago. Gas from the volcano killed around 2,000 Nisg̱a'a People, and three villages were covered by the **molten** rock.

When the ground began to rumble and lava burst from the mountain, Nisg̱a'a People believed that Ḵ'am Ligii Hahlhaahl, their Creator and Chief of Heavens was upset with them.

With the power of fire, Gwaax̱ts'agat rose from the mountains near Gitwinksihlkw and, by extending its nose, stopped the lava from travelling farther down the river. The naxnok saved many lives.

Only a dancer from one family in the Lax̱gibuu (Wolf) tribe could wear this mask.

Some *adaawak* (stories) belong to families, while others are shared by all Nisg̱a'a People. Many versions of the volcano story are told, each with a message about respecting the natural world.

As the story of the volcano was performed, a ceremonial dancer wearing this mask could extend the nose of Gwaax̱ts'agat, made from six pieces of wood connected with nails and string.

The lava field has a long, straight edge where Gwaax̱ts'agat stopped its flow with its nose. Anhluut'ukwsim Lax̱mihl Angwinga'asanskwhl Nisg̱a'a (Nisg̱a'a Memorial Lava Bed Park) is a sacred place for Nisg̱a'a People.

JUST THE FACTS

WHAT IS IT? A *halayt* (spiritual healer) travels in a canoe in this woodcarving stained with red ochre. Halayt had supernatural powers. They could travel between the spiritual and physical worlds and had the ability to cure sickness.

WHAT DOES IT LOOK LIKE? Halayt wore crowns made of bear claws like this figure. At the front and back of the canoe are paired spirit animals that guide his way. Can you tell what animals are guiding this halayt?

WHERE DOES IT COME FROM? A museum collector who visited Laxgalts'ap in 1905 bought this carving, along with other carvings and charms belonging to a halayt. This took place when missionaries and government agents were actively discouraging traditional Nisga'a spiritual practices.

WHAT'S ITS STORY? Certain knowledge was only known to a halayt. This carving may have been used in training an apprentice, or assisted a halayt in transitioning to the spirit world.

Image by Gary Fiegehen, courtesy Nisga'a Lisims Government.

GALKSI-YOXKW HALAYT (HALAYT ON A JOURNEY)

Tell Me More

Amgat (halayt **initiates**) were often found as children, but a person could be summoned from the spirit world at any time in their life. Halayt powers were drawn from the natural world and developed through visions and dreams, revealed to them by K̲'am Ligii Hahlhaahl, the Chief of Heavens. In these dreams, their individual spirit helpers were revealed to them. Spirit helpers assisted the halayt in their travels to and from the supernatural world. Likely for that reason, they were often animals that could be seen to travel between worlds, like otters (water/land), diving birds (air/water), and bears (land/underworld). Representations of spirit helpers were carved on the items a halayt used.

WOULD YOU BELIEVE?

To summon their powers, halayt would enter into a trance state. In some ceremonies, halayt helpers called sigits'oon *would operate mechanical puppets, masks with moveable eyes and twirling headdresses, and other theatrical props to reflect the presence of spirits and the power of the halayt in a dramatic way. Halayt only worked with good spirits. Despite colonial pressures to abandon these traditional healing ways, there are still practising halayt.*

My Turn

Why do you think it's important for visitors to museums to understand that every human-made object belonged (and maybe still belongs) to a person or family?

CONNECTIONS

For many years, the government and Christian missionaries forbade Nisga'a People from practising their ceremonies and traditions, and speaking their language. Yet their cultural belongings, like this carving of galksi-yoxkw halayt, were valued by non-Indigenous collectors. Museums displayed and continue to display them as objects of art, or organize them by type, exhibiting multiple rattles together, for example. When non-Indigenous people see these pieces at a museum, they don't necessarily understand they belonged to people with specific roles. At the Nisga'a Museum, wherever possible, the belongings of individual halayt are displayed together, and their identities are reconnected through the *adaawak* (stories) that are shared.

WHY IS THIS CARVING OF A HALAYT ON A JOURNEY IMPORTANT IN THIS AREA?

Most of the cultural belongings that Nisga'a Elders selected to return to the Nass Valley through the Nisga'a Treaty relate to the clothing and special equipment of the halayt. In addition to *amhalayt hlakshl lik'inskw* (grizzly bear claw crowns), halayt wore *gwiis ul* (bearskin robes), *luux* (neck rings) of red cedar, and an *ambilaan* (apron) decorated with mountain goat hooves, puffin beaks, or charms of animal bone and teeth. Halayt worked closely with their own artists to craft their *it'iskw* (charms), *haseex* (rattle), *si'amiilukwhl an'unhl sigits'oon* (puppets), and other items they used in their healing practices. Collectors took most of these belongings as sets, likely related to an individual halayt. Since their return, these sets of belongings have been displayed together for the first time in over 100 years.

JUST THE FACTS

WHAT IS IT? This *haṁootkw* (soul catcher) was used by a halayt (spiritual healer).

WHAT DOES IT LOOK LIKE? Often carved from the leg bone of a bear, this haṁootkw is carved from an antler. The carver shows a human figure in the centre, with two open-mouthed animals at either end. The carving is inset with **abalone** and hung from a piece of hide around the wearer's neck.

WHERE DOES IT COME FROM? This soul catcher belonged to Sim'oogit (Chief) Waathl. It was **acquired** by a museum collector from his grandson Sim'oogit Ksdiyaawak, of the traditional village of Gitlaxt'aamiks in 1908.

WHAT'S ITS STORY? Chief Waathl used this soul catcher in the mid-1800s. In addition to this soul catcher, his belongings included a bear claw crown, a headdress of bear's ears, and bone head scratchers that are exhibited together.

Image by Gary Fiegehen, courtesy Nisga'a Lisims Government.

> HLI GOOTHL WILP-ADOḴSHL NISG̱A'A (NISG̱A'A MUSEUM)

HAṀOOTKW (SOUL CATCHER)

Tell Me More

When a person became ill, and couldn't be cured with natural medicines that grow in the Nass Valley, spiritual healers were called. Sickness could mean a person's soul was out of **equilibrium** or separated from the body. Through singing, chanting, and with spirit helpers, a halayt could enter the supernatural world to search for the person's soul. Once caught in the haṁootkw, strands of cedar bark were used to plug each end to guarantee the soul did not escape. **Remanifesting** in the physical world, the halayt would place the soul catcher around the patient's neck to return their soul to them. Can you see the strands of cedar?

WOULD YOU BELIEVE?

Halayt could be men or women. In addition to it'iskw *(charms) from halayt gear that depict women, there are also* si'amiilukwhl an'unhl sigits'oon *(puppets) representing female halayt. One puppet at Nisga'a Museum shows a woman with a labret, a disk of wood, bone, or shell that is placed into a puncture of the lower lip of high-ranking women.*

My Turn

In your world, which is highly technological, how do you create a balance with nature and your own environment?

CONNECTIONS

Early missionaries viewed the secretive and special knowledge of halayt to be devil's work. Many halayt stopped practising because of pressure from the church and government agents. But the power of halayt and their ceremonial gear may be why halayt and their families chose to sell their belongings to museum collectors as sets, rather than see them split apart or destroyed. It was very important to Nisga'a Elders, who helped plan the museum and who experienced or heard stories of the power of halayt for healing, to make sure these belongings returned home to the Nass Valley. Repatriation is a form of healing the wrongs of colonialism, as is the return of belongings so closely tied to the Nisga'a **philosophy** of health as a state of equilibrium.

WHY IS THE HAMOOTKW IMPORTANT IN THIS AREA?

For Nisga'a People, to be at peace and in harmony with the world around you is to be in good health. Nisga'a strive to live in balance with the people and spirits that share their environment. Spirits live in all the animals and plants of the Nass Valley and in its mountains and rivers. From this rich environment is the **sustenance** for people's physical and spiritual selves. When these parts of a person's being are not well nourished, there is an imbalance that can **dislodge** their soul.

JUST THE FACTS

WHAT IS IT? This haseex (also called a Raven rattle) was part of the ceremonial regalia of a sim'oogit (Chief).

WHAT DOES IT LOOK LIKE? A haseexhl sim'oogit (Chief's rattle) is **intricately** carved. The main shape of the rattle is a raven, with a spirit bird on the raven's belly. Each haseex is different but many show on the raven's back a **reclining** man with a frog holding his tongue. Another bird, in the form of a mask, is located at the man's feet.

WHERE DOES IT COME FROM? This haseex may have belonged to Sim'oogit James Ksdiyaawak from the village of Gitlaxt'aamiks.

WHAT'S ITS STORY? By 1908, Sim'oogit Ksdiyaawak sold many of his chiefly possessions and those of his grandfather, Sim'oogit Waathl, who was a halayt. From letters between museum collectors and local settlers, we know there are belongings Sim'oogit Ksdiyaawak did not want to sell.

Image by Gary Fiegehen, courtesy Nisga'a Lisims Government.

Northwestern BC

> HLI GOOTHL WILP-ADOKSHL NISGA'A (NISGA'A MUSEUM)

HASEEXHL SIM'OOGIT (CHIEF'S RATTLE)

Tell Me More

In 1903, Sim'oogit Ksdiyaawak posed for a photograph in his ceremonial regalia with a Raven haseex in each hand. He is wearing an *amhalayt* (headdress) and a *gwiis halayt* (**Chilkat** robe). He stands on a *hoohlgan* (bentwood box) and is surrounded by prized belongings of his house, including many naxnok masks. Staged photos like this one were intended to **document** ways of life among Indigenous Peoples. Yet, at the same time, laws were passed to discourage traditional practices. While museum collectors or their representatives took many pictures, Ts'msyen (Tsimshian) photographer B.A. Haldane captured the image.

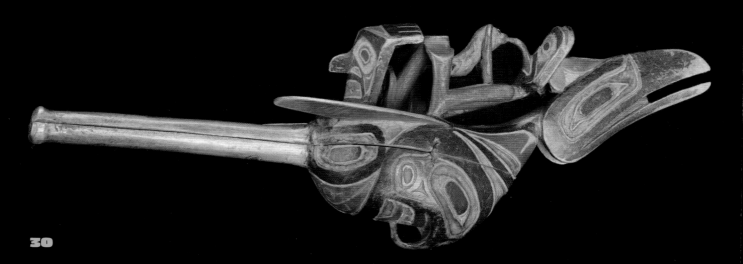

30

WOULD YOU BELIEVE?

When in use, the Raven haseex was properly held with the belly side up. In this position, on some rattles, another supernatural being is formed with the handle as its long beak, creating a direct connection between the sim'oogit and the power of the naxnok.

My Turn

Stories, skills, and knowledge passed down from great-grandparents, grandparents, and other older adults are very important. What have you learned from an older adult that you would like to pass down to the younger generation one day?

CONNECTIONS

Today, high-ranking Simgigat (Chiefs) use a carved talking stick to represent their role and to show their lineage. The talking stick will often portray the *pdeek* (tribe) and *ayukws* (family crests) of the Hereditary Chief who uses it. Traditionally, a Chief's lineage was shared on a *pts'aan* (Totem Pole) raised in front of his Longhouse. Missionaries misinterpreted house poles as a form of idol worship and forced Nisga'a People to cut them down. In some cases, collectors came into villages and harvested the pts'aan to sell to museums. The Raven haseex was used by all Nisga'a Chiefs. When Nisga'a People were not permitted to maintain their carving traditions, the specialized skill needed to make a Raven haseex was lost. Some carvers today have studied the belongings of their ancestors in order to relearn this knowledge. The new tradition of using a talking stick is a way for a sim'oogit to carry their lineage with them. Notice how each of these belongings tells more than one story.

WHY IS THE HASEEXHL SIM'OOGIT (CHIEF'S RATTLE) IMPORTANT IN THIS AREA?

The distinctive noise made by a Raven haseex mimics the sound of the supernatural bird, Aleew, shaking water from its feathers. Aleew is a naxnok that controls the whirlpool of a sacred lake where many men and canoes were pulled under the water. In one *adaawak* (story), Aleew appeared to a very careful hunter who observed the cycles of the lake and had many successful hunts. When Aleew rose from the whirlpool, the hunter could clearly see a man and a frog on its back. To show respect for the vision he received, the hunter carved the Raven haseex, which was then used to represent the power of all Nisga'a Simgigat.

SQUAMISH-LILLOOET

SQUAMISH LÍL'WAT CULTURAL CENTRE

JUST THE FACTS

WHERE IS IT? 4584 Blackcomb Way, Whistler, BC, V8E 0Y3
(604) 964-0990
https://slcc.ca
The Squamish Líl'wat Cultural Centre (SLCC) is located in the traditional territories of the Sk̲wx̲wú7mesh and Líl'wat7úl.

ARE PHOTOGRAPHS ALLOWED?
Yes.

HOW DID IT START? The Squamish and Líl'wat Nations have coexisted respectfully as neighbours since time immemorial. The cultural centre began when the Resort Municipality of Whistler met with the Líl'wat Nation to discuss their presence in Whistler. The Líl'wat Nation then met with the Squamish Nation to discuss their shared territory in Whistler. The two Nations signed a historic Protocol Agreement in 2001, formalizing their relationship, committing to cooperation and co-management of their shared territory. The cultural centre opened in 2008; it embodies the spirit of partnership between two unique Nations and stands as testimony to their proud heritage.

WHERE HAS IT LIVED?

This beautiful cultural centre was designed and built to share the cultural knowledge of the Sk̲wx̲wú7mesh (Squamish) and Líl'wat7úl (Líl'wat) Peoples.

WHERE DO THE ITEMS COME FROM?

The Squamish Líl'wat collection is made up of community-loaned belongings, public and private grants won by the SLCC, and donations from families who live or lived near the SLCC. Most recently, community-loaned belongings were repatriated from other museums to the SLCC.

HOW HAS IT CHANGED?

The Squamish Líl'wat Cultural Centre, like all other cultural attractions, had to pivot during the COVID-19 pandemic from 2019 to 2021. The virus was still around due to the variant strains. The SLCC had to shift its focus multiple times during and after the pandemic. It hosts temporary art installations and exhibitions to highlight different artists or themes of the community.

Images courtesy Squamish Líl'wat Cultural Centre.

learn about canoes used by the Squamish Nation.

MÍMNA7 CHILD-SIZE, OCEAN-GOING CANOE K̲X̲WU7LH

Image courtesy Squamish Líl'wat Cultural Centre.

This canoe was carved by a sixth-generation canoe carver, Sesíyam Ray Natraoro of the Squamish Nation, with help from apprentices at the Squamish Líl'wat Cultural Centre.

Mímna7 means "Little One" in the Squamish language. This canoe was made especially for children to interact with.

A blessing is done for all large projects made with cedar to breathe life back into the piece. After the blessing, the pieces are considered living beings who are highly respected.

A canoe out of water is considered to be sleeping. No one is to sit in it at this time. The Squamish Nation has ceremonies to put it to sleep and wake it up.

Mímna7 has not had the ceremony to breathe life back into it, so children can play and experience sitting in a canoe and have a connection to cedar.

The head is carved as a deer head to represent the canoe carver's family. It projects in front of the canoe to help it cut through ocean waves.

Cedar is known as the "Tree of Life." The Squamish Nation makes just about everything out of it: art (carving), baskets, canoes, clothes, houses, and tools.

The ocean-going canoe was used for short and long trips. The Squamish Nation still uses them for recreation travel to connect children to the protocols and procedures used to keep safe.

JUST THE FACTS

WHAT IS IT? This is regalia, traditional clothing of the Líl'wat Nation.

WHAT DOES IT LOOK LIKE? This regalia look like clothing.

WHERE DOES IT COME FROM? It was made by Sutikem Bikadi of the Líl'wat Nation.

WHAT'S ITS STORY? It's clothing that was worn by Líl'wat People before Canada was a country. Now it's worn for ceremonies and celebrations.

› SQUAMISH LÍL'WAT CULTURAL CENTRE

LÍL'WAT NATION REGALIA

Left to right: Sutikem Bikadi, Qawám Redmond Andrews, Ax7wíl Travis Billy, Swisk Jay Natrell, Telaysaht Aerienna Bruce, Téc Georgina Dan.
Image courtesy Squamish Líl'wat Cultural Centre.

WOULD YOU BELIEVE?

When working with buckskin clothing, using the traditional method of hand lacing the garment will help it last longer. While there are industrial sewing machines that can be used, the thread is thin and sharp. It will eventually tear through the buckskin.

Tell Me More

The clothing of the Lil'wat Nation was vital for keeping people warm during the long winters. The animal hide could be processed to be soft, supple, and to have some water resistance. The clothing is decorated with fringe, fur, and shells found far from home. In times where every moment was spent ensuring health and comfort during the winter, the decoration represented a family's wealth by demonstrating their ability to travel and trade for items far from home.

My Turn

Why do skins make such excellent winter clothing?

CONNECTIONS

The regalia are important to the Lil'wat Nation because they connect the people to their past. This clothing also connects them to their future because a young woman in her 20s made these pieces. By supporting young artists, the Nation is passing on its culture. It's like a relay race. The people accept the baton (culture) from their Elders and pass it on to their youth. The traditional clothing was made from animals hunted for food. As much of the animal as possible is used, so nothing is wasted to show respect to the animal for giving up its life. The Lil'wat Nation lived their lives in balance with the animals, flora, fauna, and the land itself, ensuring the health of their people.

WHY IS THE REGALIA IMPORTANT IN THIS AREA?

Regalia are important to have and wear because they connect the Nation to how its ancestors lived. It's proof of how the people adapted to the land and survived the weather. Regalia represent each family's history, stories, rights and responsibilities, and place in the community.

TL'AK̲TAX̲EN LAM (SQUAMISH NATION'S LONGHOUSE)

JUST THE FACTS

WHAT IS IT? The Tl'ak̲tax̲en lam is the traditional Longhouse of the Squamish People.

WHAT DOES IT LOOK LIKE? It was made from cedar uprights and planks tied to those uprights. Lichen was mixed with clay and packed between the planks for insulation.

WHERE DOES IT COME FROM? This Longhouse was built for the cultural centre.

WHAT'S ITS STORY? The Tl'ak̲tax̲en lam was the year-round home of the Squamish People. Many closely related family members would share the Longhouse, with their own living space divided by mats hanging from the rafters. The style of the Tl'ak̲tax̲en lam is called "shed style" because it looks like a long shed with a roof that slants in one direction. The door of the Tl'ak̲tax̲en lam always faced east. Once the rising sun hit the doorway, the family knew it was time to get up and get to work.

Tell Me More

The Tl'ak̲tax̲en lam is a very smart design because, as the extended family grew, they simply put an addition onto the end of the house. This is one reason the house was called a Longhouse. Of course, there were fires inside the Longhouse for cooking and heating. Above each firepit would be a small, separate roof facing in the opposite direction. In the lower end of this roof would be the smoke hole. Because this roof faced the opposite direction to the main roof, snow and rain couldn't get in.

Image courtesy Squamish Lil'wat Cultural Centre.

WOULD YOU BELIEVE?

The Tl'aktaxen lam is portable. When families moved from a winter site to a summer site to gather food and resources, the roofing and the planks that were tied to the upright poles could be taken off, stacked, and moved to the new location. This saved hours of labour because these boards did not need to be cut again. The support beams would stay behind for when they returned.

My Turn

What other types of housing are portable and easy to move?

The Tl'aktaxen lam shows visitors how the Squamish People worked in harmony with their land, resources, and climate. They designed houses that stayed warm and dry in the wet coastal weather and could easily be added to and reused housing materials, preserving natural resources. Talk about the ultimate recyclers!

⭐ WHY IS THE TL'A̱KTA̱XEN LAM IMPORTANT IN THIS AREA?

The Squamish Nation territory is now a big city, and their territory has changed a lot. When visitors see the Longhouse at the cultural centre, they learn about the design and building skills the Squamish People developed over thousands of years, and they can see how the family units lived together and supported each other.

Image courtesy Squamish Lil'wat Cultural Centre.

JUST THE FACTS

WHAT IS IT? The S7ístken was the traditional winter home of the Líl'wat People.

WHAT DOES IT LOOK LIKE? Members of the community came together and dug a hole about two metres deep and eight metres wide. The walls were packed with clay for insulation, and rafters made from tree branches created a conical or cone-shaped roof.

WHERE DOES IT COME FROM? The S7ístken you see here was built for the cultural centre so visitors could understand how Líl'wat ancestors lived in the long ago.

WHAT'S ITS STORY? From the outside, the S7ístken looked like part of the landscape because the rafters of its roof were packed with earth and grass that kept the people inside warm in the winter and cool in the summer. These living roofs made the houses almost invisible so enemies would have a hard time finding them.

Tell Me More

An opening in the roof did double duty. It let out smoke from the fire used for cooking and heating, but it was also an entrance. A cedar log with notches burned into it was used as a ladder, but the last two steps were purposely left off. If an intruder tried to come down the ladder, they would fall, and everyone would know they were there. Another secret entrance was built into the side of the S7ístken for children and Elders.

Image courtesy Squamish Líl'wat Cultural Centre.

S7ÍSTKEN (LÍL'WAT PIT HOUSE)

WOULD YOU BELIEVE?

A cooking fire was lit for an hour in the morning and an hour in the evening. Women filled watertight baskets with water and placed hot rocks into these baskets to cook their meals. The heat generated from the fires kept the S7ístken warm all day and night.

My Turn

List as many advantages as you can think of for this type of communal living. Can you think of some disadvantages?

CONNECTIONS

The S7ístken is a great example of how the people connected to the land, and how they understood how to harness the natural materials to survive the long, cold winters and where to build so their homes wouldn't flood. They were using technology that many are now looking at as examples of how to live green.

Image courtesy Squamish Líl'wat Cultural Centre.

⭐ WHY IS THE S7ÍSTKEN IMPORTANT IN THIS AREA?

This S7ístken shows visitors how the Líl'wat People lived in harmony with the land. An S7ístken could hold up to 30 people. Family members slept on raised platforms around the edges of the house, using cedar boughs and pounded inner cedar strips for mattresses. They made blankets from the hides of goats and other animals. Each family group, including grandparents and grown children with their own families, had their own space. They hung dividers for privacy. You can see an example of a divider hanging from the ceiling at the cultural centre. A larger S7ístken used for community gatherings was built at the centre, with smaller family houses built around it.

SUNSHINE COAST

SUNSHINE COAST MUSEUM & ARCHIVES

Image courtesy Tayu Hayward.

JUST THE FACTS

WHERE IS IT? 716 Winn Road, Gibsons, BC, V0N 1V0
(604) 886-8232
www.sunshinecoastmuseum.ca
Located on the unceded, traditional territory of the
Skwxwú7mesh and shíshálh Nations.

ARE PHOTOGRAPHS ALLOWED? Yes, photography is allowed, as
long as you don't use a flash!

HOW DID IT START? In 2002, the Elphinstone Pioneer Museum
and Sunshine Coast Maritime Museum joined forces to
become the Sunshine Coast Museum & Archives (SCMA).
The idea for a coast-wide museum started as a way for
both museums to do a better job presenting local heritage
by working together. Like two superheroes joining forces,
together the new SCMA could share resources, create
collaborative exhibits, and work on bigger projects.

Images courtesy SCMA staff.

WHERE HAS IT LIVED?

In the early days of the Elphinstone Pioneer Museum (1960s),
the collection was kept in the basement of Les Peterson's house
in Gibsons. Les was one of the founders of the museum society.
Eventually, the collection was moved to the basement of the
Gibsons town hall, where it was housed until 1974, when a
new museum building was built. In the 1980s, the Sunshine
Coast Maritime Museum was founded by a group of maritime
enthusiasts who operated a museum overlooking the ocean in
Gibsons. Today's museum has two floors of exhibits, archival and
artifact storage rooms, and a **reference library**. The outside of the
building features a beautiful mural of the Sunshine Coast by local
artist Jan Poynter.

WHERE DO THE ITEMS COME FROM?

The community donated most of the collection. These artifacts
tell important stories about the people, places, and events on the
Sunshine Coast. Sometimes objects from the coast will travel to
far-off places, so friendly donors will get in touch and send them
back. Other times important cultural artifacts are repatriated
back to the Skwxwú7mesh and shíshálh Nations. Today, the
museum has over 7,500 artifacts!

HOW HAS IT CHANGED?

When the museum formalized its role as the regional heritage
museum for the lower Sunshine Coast, it became responsible
for presenting and preserving the diverse histories from a large
area. As it is located in both Skwxwú7mesh and shíshálh Nation
territory, it also meant that the museum began to work more
collaboratively on **co-curated** exhibits and event programming.

learn from Jess Silvey, a well-known shíshálh Nation weaver and Knowledge Keeper.

SHÍSHÁLH NATION BASKET

In shíshálh culture, cedar baskets are very important. They are used for many purposes, including food gathering, berry picking, storage, and transportation. Baskets are also used to trade for other items.

shíshálh Nation Knowledge Keeper Basil Joe donated this item to the museum.

This basket was created after European contact and tells an important story about survival. As residential school and government legislation attempted to extinguish First Nations cultures, many shíshálh women took up the practice of basket weaving.

The basket was woven by telesulwit, who was Basil's grandmother. telesulwit was born in the early 1800s, or even earlier.

As a weaver and Knowledge Keeper, Jess spoke about how "cedar bark is so important to the shíshálh as a people."

Jess says that, traditionally, only a few women would be weavers, but in order to survive, baskets were made for "the tourist trade" and sold to settlers.

This basket is important as it represents the survival of shíshálh weaving culture, an art that has existed here since time immemorial.

Jess describes how cedar is a gift from the Creator, used for many purposes, including basket making.

JUST THE FACTS

WHAT IS IT? This is a decorative glass oil lamp.

WHAT DOES IT LOOK LIKE? The base of the lamp is turquoise blue and decorated with pressed flowers. The amber-tinted glass at the top of the lamp contains the oil for burning. The wick at the top is used to light the lamp.

WHERE DOES IT COME FROM? The Gibson family donated it.

WHAT'S ITS STORY? Early settler Charlotte Gibson brought this lamp with her from Ontario to Átl'ka7tsem (Howe Sound) in 1886. The lamp was used to light a salon or dining room in the Gibsons' house before there was electricity on the coast. Charlotte was a midwife and she also used it for light when she was delivering babies. Between 1889 and 1903, Charlotte delivered 15 babies, eight of which were her grandchildren. Most midwives during that time were paid through the barter system – this means instead of using money, they were traded a service or some goods for their work.

> SUNSHINE COAST MUSEUM & ARCHIVES

CHARLOTTE GIBSON'S LAMP

Tell Me More

Charlotte was known in her community for her hard work, selflessness, and nursing skill. In 1892, when a local man called Arthur Hyde became sick with smallpox, it was Charlotte who looked after him. This was very brave as the deadly disease was highly **contagious**. Smallpox causes a great deal of suffering. Survivors are often left badly scarred or blinded. Soon she and everyone in her family, with the exception of her son Ralph, were ill. It's not clear if the Gibson family had been vaccinated, but everyone survived, though Charlotte's daughter, Lottie, almost died.

My Turn

Make your own lava lamp! Start with a jar, water, vegetable oil, food colouring, Alka-Seltzer tablets, and a spoon.

1. Fill the jar with water about 1/3 of the way full.
2. Put in 45 ml of food colouring.
3. Fill the rest of the jar with cooking oil.
4. Crumble an Alka-Seltzer tablet into your jar.
5. Now watch your lava lamp bubble.

 **CONNECTIONS**

Just like nowadays with the vaccines against COVID-19, when Dr. Edward Jenner introduced the world's first vaccine against smallpox, many people were doubtful. They didn't understand how it could work. People were frightened. This was an illness that had been killing people for 800 years. Some people thought because the **inoculant** was made using **cowpox** virus that it would turn them into a cow. This may seem weird to us, but remember in the 19th century people really didn't understand how diseases were spread.

 WHY IS THE LAMP IMPORTANT IN THIS AREA?

This lamp represents a time before the use of electricity shaped the lives of settlers on the Sunshine Coast. Imagine Charlotte Gibson helping to deliver babies in the early settler community of Gibsons by the light of this beautiful lamp! The turquoise-coloured glass must have look magical when the lamp was lit.

JUST THE FACTS

› SUNSHINE COAST MUSEUM & ARCHIVES
JADE MONKEY

WHAT IS IT? This is a carving of a monkey made out of jade.

WHAT DOES IT LOOK LIKE? The monkey has a hole in the bottom and was likely part of a set of three monkeys who sat on a stand to symbolize the traditional Japanese **proverb**, "See no evil, hear no evil, speak no evil."

WHERE DOES IT COME FROM? Charles Wyton, who inherited it from his father, Edward, donated the item.

WHAT'S ITS STORY? Part of the jade monkey's fascinating story is that it was found in May 1920, under a tree stump in Gibsons. Nobody knows who put the monkey there or why. What happened to the other two monkeys from the set? Who did it originally belong to? The jade monkey is one of the museum's most intriguing artifacts because of the mysterious way it was found!

Tell Me More

The monkey's hands cover its mouth, representing the "speak no evil" part of the proverb. The monkey's name is Iwazaru. His job is to remind people of another old saying: "If you don't have anything nice to say, don't say anything at all." The other two monkeys are Kikazaru and Mizaru. Kikazaru is depicted with his hands over his ears, which represents "hear no evil." Mizaru covers his eyes to demonstrate "see no evil." The proverb came to Japan a long, long time ago. The thought is it travelled from India to Japan by way of Buddhist monks from China around the eighth century. The set serves as a reminder to live a positive life.

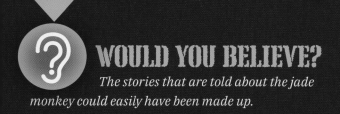

WOULD YOU BELIEVE?

The stories that are told about the jade monkey could easily have been made up.

My Turn

Is there something you feel strongly about? Do you have a cause you want others to know about? Why not make a piece of art to express how you feel? You can sing, dance, draw, write – it doesn't matter how you tell your story as long as you get your ideas out there.

CONNECTIONS

Mahatma Gandhi is often called the Father of India. He was a politician who worked hard to unite all the people of India despite their differences. As a leader in India's fight for independence from British rule, he encouraged nonviolent protest. This means Gandhi told protestors to practise civil disobedience instead of physically fighting. An example of this is he and his followers walked 388 kilometres to collect salt rather than buy British salt and pay their taxes. This may not seem like a big deal, but it was against the law for Indians to make or sell salt.

Gandhi was not a man for possessions. He kept only very few items, but among them was a statue of the three monkeys. This stirred the imagination of the Indian artist, Gupta, and inspired his sculpture series, *Gandhi's Three Monkeys*. Created in 2008, the artwork focuses on Gandhi's devotion to peacefully working against injustice.

WHY IS THE JADE MONKEY IMPORTANT IN THIS AREA?

The jade monkey is an important artifact because of its ties to Japanese culture on the Sunshine Coast. There is a rich history of Japanese fishers and loggers in the area going back to the early 1900s, but we do not have many artifacts to tell their stories. When the Japanese Canadian Internment happened in 1942 during the Second World War, all the Japanese residents were taken away and their belongings were **confiscated** and sold.

Sunshine Coast

QATHET MUSEUM & ARCHIVES

JUST THE FACTS

WHERE IS IT? 4790 Marine Avenue, Powell River, BC, V8A 4Z5
(604) 485-2222
www.qathetmuseum.ca
The qathet Museum & Archives is located on traditional
territories of the Tla'amin Nation. *qathet* means "working
together."

ARE PHOTOGRAPHS ALLOWED?
Photographs are not allowed within the museum or archives.

HOW DID IT START? The idea of starting a museum was initiated
by Golden Stanley, a local Powell River resident, in the early
1960s. Born in Vancouver in 1910, and known as "Goldy" to
his friends, he'd moved to Powell River in the 1930s and found
work as logger. A man of many talents, he had an appreciation
and love of history. He, as well as like-minded community
members, began collecting and keeping items in various
basements and attics around the community in the hope that
one day a museum would be built.

WHERE HAS IT LIVED?

This museum and archives has made a few moves over the
years. In 1962, a small space became available in the city
hall building and was dedicated to the storage of artifact
and archival material under the guidance of the museum's
first president, Gordon German. This room was soon very
full, so in 1967, the administration building, also known as
the Centennial Building, was built for the express purpose
of housing the city's recreational facilities and museum's
collections. In 1971, a youth centre was built next to the
Centennial Building. Three years later, the museum took
over management of that space where today the exhibits
are housed.

WHERE DO THE ITEMS COME FROM?

Community members donated all three of the items you
will read about.

HOW HAS IT CHANGED?

As it has for over 60 years, the qathet Museum & Archives
will continue to preserve and present the qathet region's
history and heritage for the benefit of current and future
generations.

learn what people in the past ate and where they slept.

RODMAY HERITAGE HOTEL FRENCH FRY CUTTER

At Rodmay Heritage Hotel the kitchen staff used this french fry cutter to make delicious french fries for their guests.

The Rodmay was Powell River's first hotel. Originally, it was called Powell River Hotel. It officially opened in the spring of 1911.

The hotel was impressive, with gabled windows and the sloping roof of a Swiss chalet.

This is where most newcomers stayed in the early years when Powell River was just a new town.

The cutter is made of metal and is very sharp. Staff had to be careful not to cut their fingers.

The first recipe for fries was published in 1795, in *La Cuisinière Républicaine*. Imagine, the french fry is over 200 years old!

It's rumoured the hotel is haunted by five ghosts. One of them is thought to be Charlie, a Chinese Canadian cook. His ghost is the most frequently seen.

JUST THE FACTS

PRINCESS MARY STEAM WHISTLE

WHAT IS IT? This is a brass steam whistle from the *Princess Mary*, 1910–1952. A steam whistle is a device used to produce a sound by the action of steam. It's usually attached to a steam boiler. This is where the steam is created by the boiling water. Sometimes nowadays we call this the horn of a boat.

WHAT DOES IT LOOK LIKE? It looks like a large version of a toy whistle.

WHERE DOES IT COME FROM? John Campbell brought the steam whistle to the museum. A long-time mill employee, he was able to acquire it from MacMillan Bloedel Ltd. and the Powell River Company.

WHAT'S ITS STORY? Bow, McLachlan & Company, of Paisley, Scotland, built the *Princess Mary* in 1910. A passenger vessel, and part of a series of ships known as the Princess fleet, it was 75.5 metres in length and 1,727 tonnes. It was known as a "pocket liner" because it was a miniature version of a fancy ocean liner.

Tell Me More

The *Princess Mary* is remembered fondly by locals and was favoured over other ships. The vessel was very comfortable, with day accommodations as well as 59 first class cabins equipped with 118 berths and 30 additional berths in the second class. Its first route was the Nanaimo–Comox–Vancouver service. Its first day of service was on March 14, 1911. Many years later, in 1952, she was retired and was sold to the Union Steamship Company as a barge. Her **superstructure** was scrapped with the exception of her cafeteria and dining room, which became a restaurant in Victoria, the popular Princess Mary.

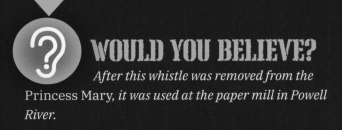

WOULD YOU BELIEVE?

After this whistle was removed from the Princess Mary, *it was used at the paper mill in Powell River.*

My Turn

Do you know how to whistle? Here's a quick lesson. Start by wetting your lips and puckering. Now slowly blow air out through your lips-gently at first. Remember to keep your tongue relaxed. Can you hear anything? Blow harder. Now experiment with different sounds using your lips, jaw, and tongue.

CONNECTIONS

Today, communities along the coast, like Powell River, are being connected to each other through BC Ferries, just like the *Princess Mary* did in her day. Each ferry has a loud whistle to signal passengers and other vessels.

WHY IS THE STEAM WHISTLE IMPORTANT IN THIS AREA?

The steam whistle represents the era of steamships, an important part of BC's past. These steamships played a crucial role, allowing travellers to reach isolated towns like Powell River. For some people living in remote areas, the steamships were their only connection with the world at large.

JUST THE FACTS

BILLY GOAT SMITH'S GRINDER

WHAT IS IT? This is a grinder made by Billy Goat Smith to be used at his cabin located at the head of Powell Lake, near Jim Brown Creek.

WHAT DOES IT LOOK LIKE? The homemade wooden grinder has a drum that is turned with a handle. Billy used it for grinding vegetables from his garden to feed his goats. His garden was known as one of the nicest in the area. He also ground apples to make cider.

WHERE DOES IT COME FROM? Martin Rossander donated it to the museum in August 1965.

WHAT'S ITS STORY? Billy Goat Smith, aka Robert Bonner Smith, came from New York state in 1910. He earned his nickname because he raised goats and hunted wild goats as well. He worked very hard to be self-sufficient and lived in his cabin as a recluse. The only way to reach his cabin was by boat.

Images courtesy qathet Museum & Archives.

WOULD YOU BELIEVE?

Billy Goat Smith is buried at Powell River Regional Cemetery (known locally as Cranberry Cemetery). His gravestone is engraved with both his real name and his nickname, as well as the emblem of a goat.

CONNECTIONS

Many people today are trying to do what Billy Goat Smith did almost 100 years ago. They are trying to be more self-sufficient. Lots of cities have community gardens where apartment dwellers can grow their own vegetables. Some people plant gardens on their balconies and on rooftops. More and more people are composting their kitchen waste. Although not all of us want to be recluses, more of us understand how important recycling is for our communities and for the environment.

⭐ WHY IS THE GRINDER IMPORTANT IN THIS AREA?

The grinder represents the settlers who came to the qathet region, not to work at the pulp and paper mill but to live independently as homesteaders working the land through **pre-emptions**.

My Turn

Do you have a nickname? If you were to give yourself one, what would it be? Here's an idea: First, begin with the word "the," followed by your favourite activity, then your favourite dessert, and finally the word "kid." For example, this writer's nickname? The Dancing Lemon Meringue Pie Kid.

Tell Me More

A sign on Billy Goat Smith's property read "Powell River People and Dogs, Please KEEP OFF." Strangers were not welcome. He would warn them by firing his rifle in the air (although he was friendly to those who brought him supplies like books, newspapers, letters, and groceries). He was an excellent hunter and worked as a hunting guide for guests staying at the Rainbow Lodge, which was owned by the Powell River Company. He also sold goat's milk and fresh meat to logging camps in the region. In 1937, after his boat was wrecked in a storm, he rarely left his cabin.

LOWER MAINLAND

MUSEUM OF VANCOUVER

Courtesy Museum of Vancouver.

JUST THE FACTS

WHERE IS IT? 1100 Chestnut Street, Vancouver, BC, V6J 3J9
(604) 736-4431
https://museumofvancouver.ca
Museum of Vancouver (MOV) is located within the unceded, ancestral territories of the xʷməθkʷəy̓əm (Musqueam), Sḵwx̱wú7mesh (Squamish), and səlilwətaɬ (Tsleil-Waututh) Nations.

ARE PHOTOGRAPHS ALLOWED? Yes, taking photos and sharing them on social media is encouraged. Tag @museumofvan.

HOW DID IT START? Over 100 years ago, some very forward-thinking people formed the Art, Historical and Scientific Association and for ten years gathered many interesting and diverse items. The association then gave its collection to the City of Vancouver. That's how the City Museum came to be.

WHERE HAS IT LIVED?

At first, the City Museum shared the Carnegie Building at Main and Hastings with the library. As the collection grew, sharing a space was no longer possible. The library moved and the museum took over the entire building. Like many museums in Canada, the City Museum moved into a new building that was built as a Centennial project. With the new building came a new name: the Centennial Museum. In 1981, the museum was renamed the Vancouver Museum.

WHERE DO THE ITEMS COME FROM?

Items come from donations, and other items are purchased for the collection.

HOW HAS IT CHANGED?

The museum still lives in the building constructed in 1967, but in 2002 a new wing was built, and in 2009 the museum was renamed the Museum of Vancouver. Beginning in the fall of 2022, MOV started talking to members of the community about how the long-term history galleries could change. The story of Vancouver isn't the story of just one people, but of many diverse communities that have contributed to the **evolution** of the city. The goal is to tell a more **holistic** story of Vancouver that includes different ways of knowing and being – both Indigenous and immigrant/settler.

...earn about trees that nourish many different animals and live for hundreds of years.

DOUGLAS FIR (*PSEUDOTSUGA MENZIESII*)

Courtesy Museum of Vancouver.

Coast Douglas firs can grow 20 to 100 metres tall. If you stacked seven transport trucks end to end on top of each other, that's about 100 metres.

ts'sá:yelhp is the name for Douglas fir in the Coast Salish Halq'eméylem (Halkomelem) language.

Before settlers arrived in Vancouver, hən'q'əmin'əm'- and Sḵwx̱wú7mesh-speaking Peoples had harvested the forests sustainably for thousands of years.

Red tree voles build nests in the branches of Douglas firs and eat the needles of the tree. Their nests can be 2–50 metres off the ground. At the tallest, that's about as high as a 16-storey building!

The Stó:lō Coast Salish People use Douglas fir to construct dip nets because the wood is strong and hard-wearing. You can learn more about dip nets by visiting the Fraser River Discovery Centre in this book.

An old story says the three-pointed bracts you can see on the tree's cones are the tails and feet of mice who were trapped inside the cones by the tree when they were greedily feeding on its seeds.

This round was cut from a log on Vancouver Island in 1968 by the forestry company MacMillan Bloedel. In the late 1960s, it was displayed in an exhibit that focused on the positive impacts of logging – job creation and economic prosperity. Its presence today in the long-term exhibition *That Which Sustains Us* is a reminder of the consequences of deforestation, such as water contamination, soil erosion, and the loss of biodiversity.

SEAL OF VANCOUVER

WHAT DOES IT LOOK LIKE? In the centre of this six-centimetre bronze seal is a railway engine beside trees. In the background are sailing ships. The words "A.D. 1886/By Sea and Land We Prosper" surround the images. The outer edge is inscribed with "City of Vancouver/British Columbia."

WHERE DOES IT COME FROM? Hugh C. Christie, a former Vancouver official, found it while cleaning out his woodshed. He donated it to the Vancouver city archives.

WHAT'S ITS STORY? Laughlin Hamilton designed this seal over 120 years ago. The city used the seal for 17 years. During a fire in city hall, the seal fell off the city clerk's desk and ended up in the basement. Hugh Christie took some of the burnt wood home with him and found the seal trapped in between pieces of wood.

Tell Me More

Official seals are used to show that a document is authentic or real. Things like birth, marriage, and death certificates all carry an official seal. Today, most seals are pressed into the paper so they can't be removed. This seal, however, is meant to be used with wax. The words and the images are carved backwards into the bronze so when the seal is pressed onto soft wax, they are the correct way around.

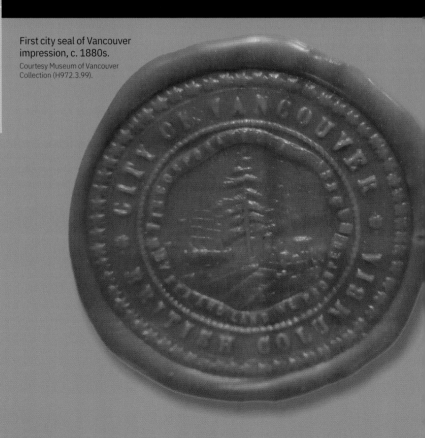

First city seal of Vancouver impression, c. 1880s.
Courtesy Museum of Vancouver Collection (H972.3.99).

CONNECTIONS

It is important to remember the past but also to understand and show how things have changed. If you look at Vancouver's coat of arms today, you will see several changes. The current motto reads, "By land, sea and air we prosper." Why do you think "air" wasn't included in the original motto? The forests and sea are now represented by a fisher and a logger. They hold a shield with a background of wavy blue and white lines that looks like the sea, two roses (the city's flower), and a Kwakwaka'wakw Totem Pole (representing First Nations). Before 1969, there was no image that showed the importance of Indigenous People to the history of the city. The sailing ship is the one image that is still seen in the modern coat of arms.

First city seal of Vancouver, c. 1880s.

WOULD YOU BELIEVE?

The designer of the first seal of Vancouver, Laughlan Hamilton, was the person who laid out and named Vancouver's streets. He even named one after himself.

My Turn

Look online to find the coat of arms for a town or city near you. What does it look like? Do you think it represents what's happening in your area in the 21st century?

WHY IS THE CITY SEAL IMPORTANT IN THIS AREA?

Firsts are always important, and this seal was the first one used for the City of Vancouver. This seal represents what was important to Vancouver. So let's look at the images. The sailing ship shows the importance of the sea. The city was and still is a major port for importing and exporting goods. Logging was an important industry in Vancouver's early days, which is why there are trees on the seal. Finally, trains connected Vancouver to the rest of the country. In order to send goods to and receive goods from the east, trains were essential. How well do you think the images support the city's motto, "By land and sea we prosper"? There's another visual symbol on this seal. Can you find it and explain why it is important?

JUST THE FACTS

WHAT IS IT? This shrine was used to store objects of religious importance.

WHAT DOES IT LOOK LIKE? It looks like a little wooden building with a roof and double doors. Inside are two of the seven gods of luck (or fortune), Ebisu and Daikoku. It is made of hinoki cypress and dates from 1800–1868.

WHERE DOES IT COME FROM? The museum purchased this shrine from an antique shop in 1993.

WHAT'S ITS STORY? When Japanese people settled in Canada, they brought with them the oldest form of Indigenous belief in Japan – Shintoism. This shrine is a Shinto shrine. Unfortunately, the story behind it is not known. Although museums find out as much as they can about items in their collections, it isn't always possible to discover the background of a belonging, where it came from, or whom it belonged to.

› MUSEUM OF VANCOUVER

SHINTO HOUSEHOLD SHRINE

Shinto household shrine.
Courtesy Museum of Vancouver Collection (DB 1454).

Tell Me More

Shintoism has been practised in Japan for time immemorial, which means before anyone can remember. Unlike most religions, there is not one person who started Shintoism. Those who follow the Shinto religion believe in many gods or spirits known as *kami*. There is no special day of the week that believers gather to worship their gods, and there is no sacred book like the Bible or the Quran. Those who follow Shinto choose when and where they want to worship the kami. People can worship at public shrines, but many set up a shrine like this one in their own homes. The household shrine is usually set high on a shelf called a *kamidana*.

WOULD YOU BELIEVE?

There are about 80,000 public Shinto shrines in Japan.

My Turn

What can you find out about Ebisu and Daikoku, the kami in this shrine? If you are using the internet, how can you tell if the sites you are visiting are reliable sources of information?

CONNECTIONS

Archeologists from Capilano University recently found the remains of a Japanese settlement in the Lower Seymore Conservation Reserve in North Vancouver. The small village was once home to 50 Japanese settlers who did not want to adopt the European culture. They brought Shintoism to their new home. For more than two decades, a shrine protected this secluded forest settlement, until it was abandoned probably in 1942 when Japanese were put into internment camps.

WHY IS THE SHINTO SHRINE IMPORTANT IN THIS AREA?

In the 1890s, Chinese and Japanese migrants began arriving in Vancouver to work in local sawmills and canneries. By 1906, workers were also arriving from India and other parts of South Asia. Many Japanese people who settled in the Vancouver area brought their beliefs with them. This meant that Shintoism came to British Columbia. Although Shintoism has followers around the world, most believers live in Japan or in areas of other countries that have a concentrated population of Japanese people.

JUST THE FACTS

WHAT IS IT? This is a cougar pelt or skin.

WHAT DOES IT LOOK LIKE? This brown and white cougar pelt includes the whiskers, claws, and even the cat's foot pads. Tip to tail, it's 180 centimetres long (about the length of your bed).

WHERE DOES IT COME FROM? Edgar Pearce, who killed the cougar around 1920, kept the pelt and his relatives donated it to the museum in 2010.

WHAT'S ITS STORY? While Kitsilano is now an urban area in Vancouver, it was once covered with dense forest. When settlers came, they set up logging camps and mills. Edgar killed the cougar when it came into a logging camp.

Tell Me More

The cougar, whose scientific name is *Puma concolor*, is also called a mountain lion and a puma. In fact, it has so many names it's in the *Guinness World Records* for having more common names (in English) than any other mammal. Can you find out how many it has? Cougars are reclusive cats, meaning people don't often see them. They are carnivores (meat eaters) that like deer, elk, and moose, but they will eat much smaller animals when necessary. Female cougars range (on average) 140 square kilometres. That's bigger than the City of Vancouver. The male's range is much larger, on average 280 square kilometres.

Lower Mainland

> **MUSEUM OF VANCOUVER**

KITSILANO COUGAR PELT

Kitsilano cougar pelt, 1919.
Courtesy Museum of Vancouver Collection (NM 286).

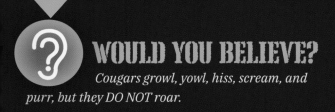

WOULD YOU BELIEVE?

Cougars growl, yowl, hiss, scream, and purr, but they DO NOT roar.

My Turn

Do cougars exist in the area around where you live? If so, what are they called? If not, what is the nearest area where cougars might live?

There are several conservation groups working hard to protect cougars (and other wildlife) by building passageways over and under highways so animals can avoid getting killed by cars and trucks. Conservationists also meet with governments and farmers to find ways to protect wilderness areas and habitat so both cougars and humans can live happily together.

WHY IS THE COUGAR IMPORTANT IN THIS AREA?

Cougars are top predators and help preserve biodiversity. They keep numbers of large herbivores like deer under control, which is important because too many herbivores gobble up vegetation that feeds many other animals and provides nesting areas for birds. When a cougar kills, the leftovers become part of the food chain. Smaller mammals, like foxes, **raptors**, and many insects feed on the parts left behind. Even soil underneath the carcasses is made richer, which is great for growing new plants and trees. We humans are not helping. We keep increasing the sizes of our cities and towns and building roads and pipelines with heavy machinery, all of which decrease the habitat for this species. As their habitat decreases, cougars will come into urban areas and kill cats and dogs. This ends sadly, not only for the pets but also for the cougars that sometimes must be put down.

JUST THE FACTS

WHAT IS IT? This wooden sculpture shows a man cradling a salmon in his arms. This figure welcomed the annual salmon runs at Pukwayúsem, a Skwxwú7mesh (Squamish) village at the junction of the Squamish and Cheakamus rivers.

WHAT DOES IT LOOK LIKE? Made from painted red cedar, Wáx̱ayus is around 147 centimetres tall. He was hand-carved with an adze.

WHERE DOES IT COME FROM? An Indian agent sold the sculpture to the museum in 1929 after collecting it from Pukwayúsem. Museums now recognize that belongings taken from Indigenous Peoples between the 1830s and 1960s were not given willingly.

WHAT'S ITS STORY? Xats'alanexw-t (August Jack Khahtsahlano) carved Wáx̱ayus in the 1920s to replace an older version. The original would have been made about the time your great-great-great-great-grandparents lived, which was a long time ago.

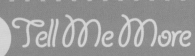

Tell Me More

When people needed special carvings made, like welcome figures, they asked people who specialized in those areas. Carving was an occupation, just like canoe making and weaving. Sometimes they hired someone who did not live in their village. This is how Xats'alanexw-t came to make this welcome figure for a Squamish member of Pukwayúsem. Xats'alanexw-t was a resident of the village of Sen̓áḵw, which is where the Museum of Vancouver now stands, on the shores of False Creek.

WÁX̱AYUS, WELCOMING SALMON

Wáx̱ayus Salmon Chief figure.
Courtesy Museum of Vancouver Collection (AA 687).

WOULD YOU BELIEVE?

Burrard Inlet was once rich with herring and other fish, but pollution destroyed their habitats. Recent efforts to restore eelgrass beds and wrap creosote pilings with special netting increase survival of fish eggs. These types of projects have helped both herring and salmon to be successful in the city. More fish has led to whales reappearing in local waters.

My Turn

For decades, the Museum of Vancouver and other BC museums have been repatriating belongings wrongfully removed from Indigenous communities. In 2023, two Totem Poles were repatriated in BC. Using the internet, find stories about belongings that have been repatriated to Indigenous Peoples.

CONNECTIONS

Before settlers came to the Vancouver area, the village of Seṅáḵw, located in what is now called False Creek, was a home to Skwx̱wú7mesh families. The people hunted deer, elk, and beaver, and fished for salmon. They built Longhouses and held Potlatches. As settlers started to move into the area, the federal government set aside almost 50 hectares of land on False Creek in 1869 as the Kitsilano Indian Reserve. In 1877, Seṅáḵw, now part of Kitsilano IR#6, was set aside for the Skwx̱wú7mesh community only. City building led to loss of biodiversity and traditional hunting and fishing grounds began to disappear. Thirty-six years later, Skwx̱wú7mesh families were forced off the land and the village was burned. As the city grew, so did the amount of pollution in creeks feeding the Fraser River. Many streams where salmon used to spawn disappeared under concrete and asphalt.

WHY IS WÁX̱AYUS IMPORTANT IN THIS AREA?

The fish Wáx̱ayus holds shows us the importance of salmon to the Skwx̱wú7mesh Nation. Salmon are a gift that must be treated with respect, and there are many oral traditions along the coast that teach this. If we do not treat the natural world and its gifts with respect, these gifts will disappear.

One of the last owned fishing sites was located in Pukwaẏúsem. A fishing site is called a *ḵtiṅ* (pool in the river). In this village there was a welcome figure as a symbol of respect for the salmon. Another way that the Skwx̱wú7mesh People show their respect for the salmon is with a First Salmon Ceremony each spring when the salmon begin to run in the rivers. A further traditional practice involves returning uneaten salmon bones to the water so the salmon will return the following season.

MUSEUM OF ANTHROPOLOGY AT UBC

JUST THE FACTS

WHERE IS IT? 6393 NW Marine Drive, Vancouver, BC, V6T 1Z2
(604) 822-5087
https://moa.ubc.ca
The Museum of Anthropology (MOA) is located on the unceded territories of the hən̓q̓əmin̓əm̓-speaking Musqueam Peoples.

ARE PHOTOGRAPHS ALLOWED? Yes, without a flash. You might enter a temporary exhibit that does not allow photos; please respect the "no photos" signs.

HOW DID IT START? The museum was established in 1949 as a unit within the Faculty of Arts at the University of British Columbia (UBC).

Images courtesy UBC Museum of Anthropology, Vancouver, Canada.

WHERE HAS IT LIVED?

The Museum of Anthropology has always been located on the unceded territories of the hən̓q̓əmin̓əm̓-speaking Musqueam Peoples. It lived in the basement of the University of British Columbia's library until 1976, when it moved to the beautiful building and grounds you see today. Famous Canadian architect Arthur Erikson designed this award-winning building, which is home to the museum and the Laboratory of Archaeology. He worked closely with landscape architect Cornelia Hahn Oberlander to create an outside space that complemented the building and was representative of the museum's large collection of northwest coast Indigenous belongings.

WHERE DO THE ITEMS COME FROM?

Museums with Indigenous collections have a difficult history, as most were created by **colonizers** and contain belongings and treasures collected as part of colonization. The works you see at the Museum of Anthropology have mostly been purchased by the museum or have been donated to it. Today, museums like MOA are examining collecting histories and working with Indigenous communities and families on repatriation. That means giving back belongings that were taken from them.

HOW HAS IT CHANGED?

In 2010, MOA underwent a major renovation and increased its size by 50 per cent. In 2017, it opened the Elspeth McConnell Gallery of Northwest Coast Masterworks. That same year, the university deemed the Great Hall at risk in the event of a significant earthquake and a plan was put in place to rebuild it. By 2020, all the objects were removed from the Great Hall. The museum staff worked with Indigenous communities and families to try and ensure that proper protocols and procedures were followed when the belongings were moved. Once the reconstruction of the Great Hall was complete, the massive carvings were reinstalled and some new ones were added. In 2024, the museum celebrated its 75th anniversary.

see how Musqueam First Nation members are still practising the weaving methods their ancestors used for thousands of years.

TEN: A MUSQUEAM HANGING

With permission from artists Debra and Robyn Sparrow (Nbz842).

Artists Debra and Robyn Sparrow named this weaving *Ten*, meaning "mother" in hən̓q̓əmin̓əm̓, the language of the Musqueam Peoples. They are honouring their mother and all mothers.

This handmade hanging was **commissioned** by the museum for the ramp that leads visitors into the museum. It was completed in 1999.

Robyn and Debra spun sheep's wool, then wove it by hand. They used modern dyes because they knew their weaving would be exposed to strong lights. Modern dyes generally fade more slowly than natural dyes.

Musqueam People have been weaving beautiful, patterned blankets for thousands of years. Traditionally, they used mountain goat hair and hair from specially bred dogs with long, white double coats.

The white dogs were kept on islands, so they did not breed with village dogs. Women would canoe out to the islands and feed the dogs a special diet of fish and marine mammals.

Weaving involved many skills, including hunting mountain goats, collecting hair from the white dogs, gathering and creating natural dyes, cleaning and protecting the hair and fur using **diatomaceous earth**, spinning, and preparing the looms, all before the weaving began.

Traditional weaving almost disappeared. Colonization forced people onto reserves where the materials weavers needed were not available. Residential schools worked to break the connection between children and their parents and grandparents, so children didn't learn to weave as part of their normal childhood activities.

JUST THE FACTS

WHAT IS IT? This is a large sculpture by Haida artist Bill Reid.

WHAT DOES IT LOOK LIKE? *The Raven and the First Men* is almost two metres tall and two metres wide. King-size beds are two metres long. A standard doorway is two metres tall. The Raven hunches on the top of a clamshell. His head is tilted to one side as if he is listening. There are six figures climbing out of the clamshell. Because people are born without clothes, you can see many bare bottoms.

WHERE DOES IT COME FROM? It was commissioned by the museum.

WHAT'S ITS STORY? Bill Reid worked on the sculpture with artists Guujaaw, James Hart, George Norris, and George Rammell. It was completed in 1980. The sculpture is so famous that, in 2004, it was on the Canadian 20 dollar bill.

Tell Me More

The sculpture was not made from one tree. There were few old-growth yellow cedar trees left that were large enough to make the carving and it was impossible to find one big enough without some rot or other defects. Instead, it was sculpted from 106 yellow cedar beams laminated together into a block weighing more than 4000 kilograms. Laminated wood is made by gluing together several layers or beams of lumber. The block was strong and wouldn't crack or twist over time. A bed of sand surrounds the sculpture that was brought by children to the museum from Rose Spit, Haida Gwaii, where Haida history tells that the Raven discovered mankind in a clamshell.

Lower Mainland

› MUSEUM OF ANTHROPOLOGY AT UBC

THE RAVEN AND THE FIRST MEN

Image courtesy Jessica Bushey, with permission from the Bill Reid Estate (Nb1.481).

WOULD YOU BELIEVE?

When Bill Reid carved The Raven Discovering Mankind in a Clamshell, *a tiny sculpture that looks much like this one, he made the people crawling out of the shell both male and female. Later, he learned the original Haida story had only men climbing from the shell, so in the large sculpture you will see only male figures.*

My Turn

How many figures can you see in the photos? Look at their body language and their faces as they crawl out of the shell into the world. What do you think each of them was feeling about this new place where they are going to live?

CONNECTIONS

The Musqueam People have lived on this same land for thousands of years. They used Point Grey as a lookout from which their warriors could see visitors and enemies approaching by sea. During the Second World War, the Canadian government was worried that Vancouver could be attacked by the Japanese. Because of its location, they thought Point Grey (where the museum now lives) would be a perfect place to put large guns. The Bill Reid Rotunda and *The Raven and the First Men* sit on top of a Second World War concrete **gun emplacement** that is underneath the floor. Arthur Erikson, the architect who designed the museum, decided to build the gun emplacement into his plans. As a result, the discovery of mankind as we see it in Bill Reid's sculpture sits on top of a place where there was a gun meant to be used in war.

WHY IS *THE RAVEN AND THE FIRST MEN* IMPORTANT IN THIS AREA?

About 20 years earlier, Bill Reid created his first monumental works, including five Totem Poles and an inside house post for the University of British Columbia carved with the help of Doug Cranmer, a skilled Kwakwa̱ka'wakw artist. He then carved a tall pole in honour of his mother's childhood home and community of Skidegate on Haida Gwaii with the assistance of young artists Guujaaw, Robert Davidson, Gerry Marks, and Joe David. As he studied and practised Haida **visual language** on large and small works, he developed his own style that we can see in both the tiny sculpture *The Raven Discovering Mankind in a Clamshell,* and the towering *The Raven and the First Men.* By the time he carved *The Raven and the First Men*, though, he had developed Parkinson's disease. With this disease, a person loses the ability to control their muscles, including muscles used for creating detailed small carvings. To complete this monumental sculpture, he again relied on a group of talented younger artists to help him.

JUST THE FACTS

WHAT IS IT? This Kwakwa̱ka̱'wakw mask represents the supernatural Ninini (earthquake).

WHAT DOES IT LOOK LIKE? The mask has a white background, black eyebrows, green around the eyes, a black band that runs down the nose, and red nostrils and lips. The mouth is outlined with white lines, like the vibrations of an earthquake. Its eyes are dark and glassy. A dancer can move both the eyebrows and lips.

WHERE DOES IT COME FROM? The name of the carver is not known for sure, but John Davis or Johnny Nolie may have created the mask before 1939. It was purchased by the museum in 1954.

WHAT'S ITS STORY? This mask was owned by Musgamakw Dzawada'enuxw (Moos-gum-agw Dzawa-duh Ay-noohw) Hereditary Chief Hector Webb of Gwa'yi (Kingcome Inlet), which is a fjord on the central coast of British Columbia. The Musgamakw Dzawada'enuxw are members of the Kwakwa̱ka̱'wakw group of Nations. When Hector Webb passed away, his wife sold the mask to the Museum of Anthropology.

My Turn

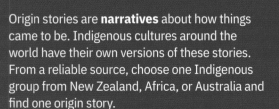

Origin stories are **narratives** about how things came to be. Indigenous cultures around the world have their own versions of these stories. From a reliable source, choose one Indigenous group from New Zealand, Africa, or Australia and find one origin story.

NININIGAMŁ (EARTHQUAKE MASK)

Image courtesy Jessica Bushey (A635).

WOULD YOU BELIEVE?

In 2019, after 60 years in the Museum of Anthropology's collection, this Ninini mask was danced in the Potlatch of Chief Gigaemi (Frank Baker) in Alert Bay. Gigaemi said of the Ninini: "I would think when he wrinkles his face that the earth wrinkles – and that would be an earthquake."

Tell Me More

Seismologists are scientists that study the vibrations beneath the earth. Every year the scientists that work with the Geological Survey of Canada record over 1,000 earthquakes in western Canada. Because Indigenous People have lived on the west coast for thousands of years, their oral histories include stories of earthquakes and tsunamis that involve supernatural beings such as Ninini. At a Kwakwaka'wakw Potlatch, Ninini is part of the Tłasila or Peace Dances (also known as family treasures). As Ninini is dancing, those watching may sway back and forth as if they have been caught in an earthquake.

CONNECTIONS

When museum staff discussed plans for the **seismic upgrade** to the Great Hall, they knew the importance of listening to and learning from the oral histories of local First Nations. They consulted Knowledge Keepers and searched the collection for belongings connected to earthquakes. Of all the First Nations masks in the collection, they found only one – Ninini. A **replica** mask carved by Les Nelson is cared for at the museum at Campbell River and can be removed by Nelson family members and their **descendants** for ceremonies.

 WHY IS THE NININI MASK IMPORTANT IN THIS AREA?

Many coastal First Nations have stories about whole villages destroyed by earthquakes and tsunamis. However, the explanations for these events are not all the same. One Nuu-chah-nulth story tells of dwarves who lived in a mountain. They invited a person to dance around their drum, but the person accidently kicked the drum and got earthquake foot. Every time he took a step, he caused an earthquake. The Nelson family from Gwa'yi (Kingcome Inlet) has the right to perform the Ninini mask, dance, and song. They hold Ninini in their box of treasures and can show this family treasure during the Tłasila portion of a Potlatch. When dancers and singers perform at ceremonies, they are showing the family's knowledge of supernatural and natural events passed down to them through their ancestors. If you enter http://www2.moa.ubc.ca/shakeupipad/#0 into your search engine on your computer, click on "Get Started" and go to "Nininigamł Earthquake Mask." There you can listen to family members talk about Ninini and see Ninini danced at a potlatch.

JUST THE FACTS

K'LCTA (SEA MONSTER MASK)

WHAT IS IT? This Nuxalk mask represents K'lcta, a sticky sea monster.

WHAT DOES IT LOOK LIKE? The face is bold, with a large green nose, red nostrils, and round cheeks. His heavy eyebrows are painted black. It's hard not to notice the bird stuck to the top of his head. Its wings are outstretched as if trying to fly away. The bird's wings and neck can be moved using strings that run down the back of the mask.

WHERE DOES IT COME FROM? This mask was probably carved by a Nuxalk artist whose name we do not know. It was purchased by the museum in 1952.

WHAT'S ITS STORY? Originally, this was thought to be a Kwakwa̱ka̱'wakw mask because the museum knew it had been used at a Kwakwa̱ka̱'wakw Potlatch. Later, it was identified as a Nuxalk mask.

Tell Me More

The mask was sold to the museum by a Kwakwa̱ka̱'wakw man and had been used at least once by a Kwakwa̱ka̱'wakw family in 1922 during a Potlatch in Tsaxis (Fort Rupert). At that Potlatch, this mask probably represented Q!umugwe', the Chief of the Undersea World. Because the mask is now known to be from the Nuxalk Nation, the figure has been identified as K'lcta. He is similar to Q!umugwe', but instead of being the Chief of the Undersea World, K'lcta is a sticky sea monster that guards the entrance to the house of Q'umukwa, the Undersea Kingdom's Chief.

Courtesy Museum of Anthropology at UBC. (A3588a) Charlie George Sr. photo Derek Tan.

WOULD YOU BELIEVE?

The word "k'lcta" means pitch or the type of sap that seeps from trees. Everything sticks to K'lcta, including the bird on his head and the salmon faces you can see on his cheeks.

My Turn

How does learning about different cultures change our understanding of the world?

Before colonization, Indigenous Peoples traded with each other, met together for different events, and married each other. So it's not a surprise that a Nuxalk mask came into a Kwakwa̱ka'wakw family and was used in their ceremonies. Families have rights that come through their ancestors or through marriage to wear certain masks, sing certain songs, and dance certain dances. When a dancer wears a mask and performs a dance during ceremonies, it tells those who are watching that the first ancestor of the family long ago met that supernatural being. Not only do songs, dances, and masks tell the family's history, they stand for the rights and **privileges** of the family. They are proof the family is allowed to gather natural resources on the land. In return, the family has the responsibility to take care of the land.

★ WHY IS THE K'LCTA MASK IMPORTANT IN THIS AREA?

In many First Nations, families hold the rights to certain stories and images. This mask was identified as K'lcta by Sxnakila Clyde Tallio, whose family holds the rights to the Undersea Kingdom story from their Nuxalk territory. Clyde recognized K'lcta as being from his family's box of treasures, so it was important that this mask, which had been carved by a Nuxalk, for a Nuxalk family to be reconnected to their original Nuxalk *smayusta* (origin story). The **curators** at the museum didn't just suddenly move the mask into the Nuxalk collection, because it had belonged to many families at different times. They worked with Kwakwa̱ka'wakw Knowledge Holders and followed **cultural protocols**. There are many Kwakwa̱ka'wakw belongings in the museum's collection and not so many from the Nuxalk. So this mask, with its distinctive look – a nice big nose, round cheeks, a certain type of blue colour – is a wonderful addition to the collection. And it has a great cross-cultural story!

JUST THE FACTS

WHAT IS IT? This is a pair of **contemporary** house posts carved by Susan Point. In the past, house posts were located inside a Longhouse and supported the beams of the house.

WHAT DOES IT LOOK LIKE? Both posts are carved from red cedar and painted. One post has a human figure with two creatures in front of it. Above its head is a red figure inside a green circle. On the second post is a figure that looks both human and bird-like. It is holding a *sʔiːɬqəy̓*, a double-headed serpent.

WHERE DOES IT COME FROM? Susan Point carved the pair. She finished them in 1997.

WHAT'S ITS STORY? They were commissioned by the Royal Bank of Canada and gifted to MOA.

Tell Me More

Susan Point was inspired by two 19th-century posts from her community that were collected for the American Museum of Natural History in New York City. This museum is over 4000 kilometres away from where the posts were carved and used. Musqueam allowed the posts to be collected so they could be used to teach visitors about the Musqueam world and who the Musqueam People are.

Image courtesy Kayla Bailey, with permission from artist Susan Point; left house post (Nbz838).

QEQƏN (MUSQUEAM HOUSE POSTS)

WOULD YOU BELIEVE?

The posts were located outside from 1997 to 2022. The artist and her family have repainted the posts to keep the colours vibrant.

My Turn

The architectural designs of traditional Indigenous houses varied depending on climate, resources, and geographical location. What can you find out about the differences between shed-style Longhouses used by the Musqueam People and Longhouses built by the Six Nations People? What other types of Indigenous architecture can you find out about? Make sure you are using reliable sources.

CONNECTIONS

Not only has Susan Point connected the place where the 19th-century posts are now located with the place where they were carved and used, but she has also connected the past with the present and the future. She has carried the Musqueam way of carving house posts into the present, and because these posts will be kept in the Great Hall, they will be preserved for all future visitors to see and learn about.

 ## WHY ARE QEQƏN IMPORTANT IN THIS AREA?

On her house posts, Susan Point makes a connection between where the 19th-century posts are now and where they came from. At the bottom of the left-hand post are waves that represent the East River that flows past Manhattan where the Natural History Museum lives. On the right-hand post are waves that stand for the Fraser River in British Columbia. She has also included the sun rising in the east (on the left-hand post) and setting in the west (on the right-hand one). Now squint and imagine the two posts pushed together. The rays of the sun become the Statue of Liberty's crown!

JUST THE FACTS

WHAT IS IT? These are hand-split red cedar boards from the front of a Tsimshian First Nation's house.

WHAT DOES IT LOOK LIKE? These boards are very old, likely from the early 1800s – older than what we now call Canada. On the surface are northwest coast designs applied with paints made with hematite, the main ore in iron that creates the colour red, and magnetite, which creates black. Magnetite is the most magnetic mineral on Earth! You could probably figure that out just by seeing its name.

WHERE DOES IT COME FROM? These boards came from Lax Kw'alaams, a village near modern-day Prince Rupert on the northern coast of BC. The family that owned them probably transported the boards as they moved from an older village to be closer to the Hudson's Bay trading post.

WHAT'S ITS STORY? In 1948, MOA purchased 22 boards that had belonged to several different houses. Two of these large boards (one is also split in two) are shown here.

› MUSEUM OF ANTHROPOLOGY AT UBC

'NIK SUUGID 'WIILEEKSM WAAP (HOUSE-FRONT BOARD)

Tell Me More

Red cedar is an important tree for coastal First Nations. It has a strong, straight grain that runs up and down the tree. This meant that people building a house could split planks off the tree using wedges and sledgehammers. They could even split off planks while the tree was still standing! The planks for the house were then finished with knives and adzes, tools originally made from stone but later from metal. Holes were drilled down the sides of the boards, and the boards were sewn together using cedar withes, which are little branchlets from the tree. The largest houses would have up to 50 relatives living inside.

Image courtesy UBC Museum of Anthropology, Vancouver, Canada.

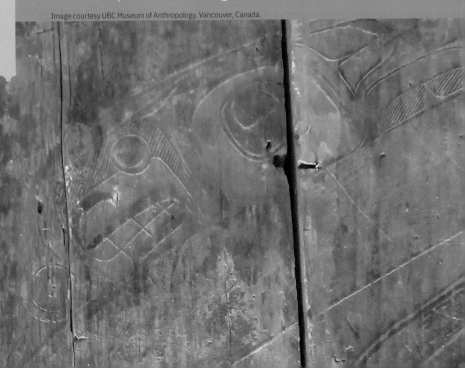

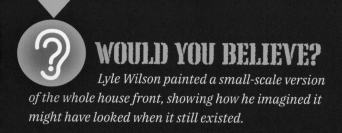

WOULD YOU BELIEVE?

Lyle Wilson painted a small-scale version of the whole house front, showing how he imagined it might have looked when it still existed.

My Turn

These house boards were not just practical but were works of art. Why is it important to preserve artworks that are hundreds and thousands of years old?

A former curator with the museum, Bill McLennan, along with Haida artist Bill Reid and Haisla artist Lyle Wilson, studied the house boards. McLennan tried a few photographic techniques (like using infrared film) to help them see the images originally painted on the house boards. These helped a bit, but then, whether by accident or on purpose, he found that when a bright light was moved across the surface, he could see the design. The boards looked like they had been shallowly carved. That's because the paint protected the wood underneath from the effects of wind, rainstorms, blowing sand, and salt air. All the unpainted areas had been eroded or worn away. First Nations artists today are learning from the discovery of these boards. The boards are like teachers about painting on such a monumental scale. And in more and more First Nations communities on the coast, new cedar-plank houses with painted fronts are being built for people to use for ceremonies and other events.

⭐ WHY IS THE 'NIK SUUGID 'WIILEEKSM WAAP IMPORTANT IN THIS AREA?

Wealthy Tsimshian Chiefs would commission artists to paint the fronts of their cedar-plank houses. Sometimes, instead of painting directly on the house, the artists would build a screen they would paint and then attach to the front. These house fronts told people who saw them who the families were: their **origins**, their history, their inherited rights and privileges. When missionaries arrived in the area, they discouraged extended families living together. They wanted each family to live in their own house like they did in Britain. Eventually, the traditional houses were taken down. The cedar planks were used to make other things or cut up for firewood. A few were collected by museums. But even when the big houses were no longer being built, people kept telling and sharing their histories and stories in other ways.

JUST THE FACTS

LEAF WITH TEXT FROM THE QURAN

WHAT IS IT? This is a leaf from the Quran, the holy book of Islam.

WHAT DOES IT LOOK LIKE? The leaf was written on vellum. That's calfskin that has been prepared so it can be used like paper. It is slightly larger than a piece of printer paper turned sideways. The words are in Kufic script, one of the earliest styles of Arabic writing.

WHERE DOES IT COME FROM? The Ismaili Muslim community donated the ancient leaf to the museum in 2013.

WHAT'S ITS STORY? There are many unanswered questions about this leaf. The exact date it was written is also unknown, but it was probably between 850 and 900 CE. That makes it over 1,000 years old!

Tell Me More

Muslims believe the Quran contains the word of God as it was spoken to the prophet Muhammad through the Angel Gabriel. Before the Quran was written down, it was memorized word for word and passed down orally. This leaf contains two complete verses and two incomplete verses. Modern versions of the Quran use numbers to show verse divisions, but the **scribe** who wrote this text used six gold discs in the shape of a triangle to show where one verse stops and another begins. The scribe stretched the letters horizontally – that's side to side – perhaps to fit the rectangular shape of the page.

Image courtesy Kayla Bailey (2988/1).

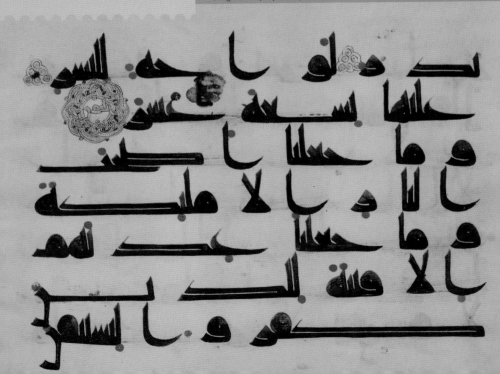

WOULD YOU BELIEVE?

Many Muslims around the world still memorize the Quran containing about 77,797 words. A person who memorizes and can recite the Quran is called a Hafiz (for males) or a Hafiza (for females). Once they have memorized the text, they must keep studying and practising so they don't forget it.

My Turn

The way Arabic is written is similar to cursive English writing, where letters are connected. Some young people have never learned cursive writing, the handwriting that their grandparents learned in school. If that's you, can you find a video online where you can learn cursive writing? Why would someone want to learn cursive writing?

CONNECTIONS

Leaves from this same copy of the Quran are found in museums and private collections around the world because they are rare and valuable pieces of Islamic history. The leaf also documents the beautiful art of Arabic **calligraphy**. Kufic script is believed to have developed in the town of Kufa, Iraq, and is used traditionally for copying the Quran and for decorating monuments. The leaf is read from right to left, since Arabic is written from right to left. Below are the same verses as in the ancient manuscript but written in modern Arabic. How are they similar? How are they different?

... لَا تَذَرُ [28] لَوَّاحَةٌ لِّلْبَشَرِ [29] عَلَيْهَا تِسْعَةَ عَشَرَ [30] وَمَا جَعَلْنَا أَصْحَابَ النَّارِ إِلَّا مَلَائِكَةً وَمَا جَعَلْنَا عِدَّتَهُمْ إِلَّا فِتْنَةً لِّلَّذِينَ كَفَرُوا لِيَسْتَيْقِنَ ...

WHY IS THE LEAF FROM THE QURAN IMPORTANT IN THIS AREA?

A holy book is always important to members of the religion to which it belongs, and this leaf comes from a very old copy of the Quran. The leaf is also interesting because of the way it looks. Not only did the scribe stretch the letters horizontally but he also left out some of the markings that tell a person **reciting** the text how to pronounce the words. Why would he do that? No one knows for sure, but some experts believe this copy of the Quran was not used for studying or recitation but displayed for its beauty. The scribe might have stretched or elongated the words and left out markings to make the page look more elegant, like a piece of sacred art. A wealthy family or a prince may have commissioned the holy book for their homes or to donate to a mosque.

JUST THE FACTS

WHAT IS IT? This is a collection of sea creatures made from discarded plastic fishing nets.

WHAT DOES IT LOOK LIKE? Each creature (turtle, hammerhead shark, jellyfish, and giant squid) hangs from the ceiling of the museum, which makes it look like it is swimming in the ocean.

WHERE DOES IT COME FROM? A group of Indigenous and non-Indigenous artists who live on Erub, a tiny island in the Torres Strait between Australia and Papua New Guinea, made these creatures. The area of Erub is 5.7 km². (To give you an idea of its size, compare the area of Prince Edward Island, Canada's smallest province, at 5660 km².) Erub is about 11,000 kilometres from Vancouver. That's twice the width of Canada!

WHAT'S ITS STORY? The museum purchased the ghost net creations between 2017 and 2020.

GHOST NET SEA CREATURES

Tell Me More

Ghost nets are plastic fishing nets that float on ocean currents. The nets may have been damaged and are unusable, or simply abandoned. Sadly, many marine animals such as turtles and sharks get caught in these nets and die. The nets also get tangled in reefs, smothering the coral. A group of artists from the island of Erub wanted to draw attention to the destruction caused by the ghost nets and started creating the sea creatures that were caught in the nets out of the same material they were trapped in.

With permission from Erub Arts Collaborative (3286/1). Image courtesy Alina Ilyasova.

WOULD YOU BELIEVE?

According to her creators, the turtle you can see in the museum is a middle-sized teenager. Her Erub name is Eip Kor Korr.

My Turn

Make a list of everything you have eaten in the last 24 hours. What packaging was used for the things you ate? What was the packaging made of? How much of it was recyclable? What happens to the packaging that isn't recyclable?

With permission from Erub Arts Collaborative (32854 3285/1 3285/2 3285/3 33081). Image courtesy Alina Ilyasova.

CONNECTIONS

Because Erub is an island, the sea and the marine animals that live there play an important part in the physical, spiritual, and cultural lives of the Indigenous People. Turtles are a major food source for Erub Islanders, but sea turtles represent 80 per cent of the marine animals captured in ghost nets. For many families, the hammerhead shark is a totem passed down from their ancestors. Removing ghost nets from the waters around the island and on the Great Barrier Reef helps to prevent the unnecessary deaths of the hammerhead shark and other marine animals. By making art and displaying their ghost net sculptures in museums around the world, the Erub Islanders are sending a message about recycling, conservation, and plastic pollution that we all should pay attention to.

⭐ WHY ARE THE GHOST NET SEA CREATURES IMPORTANT IN THIS AREA?

Although the artists who created these ghost net figures live very far away from British Columbia, their message is an important one. Ghost nets are commonly found off BC's coast. They trap fish, marine mammals, even birds. And because the nets are plastic, they contribute to the amount of plastic pollution found in the ocean. So, while these beautiful ghost net sea creatures were crafted very far from British Columbia, they remind us that discarded fishing gear is a problem, not only in a place we may never have heard of but right here in Canada.

HISTORIC JOY KOGAWA HOUSE

JUST THE FACTS

WHERE IS IT? 1450 West 64th Avenue, Vancouver, BC, V6P 2N4
(604) 897-7438
https://www.kogawahouse.com/wp/
The Marpole area of Vancouver is also called c̓əsnaʔəm by the Musqueam People who have lived here and looked after this land for thousands of years.

ARE PHOTOGRAPHS ALLOWED? Yes.

HOW DID IT START? The house was home to Japanese Canadian author Joy Kogawa and her family until it was confiscated during the Second World War and sold without the family's permission. The house is an important reminder of the **racial discrimination** this **minority** faced throughout the war and afterward. The house features in Joy's **semi-autobiographical** novel *Obasan*, which tells the story of the Japanese Canadian Internment from a child's viewpoint. Joy adapted this book for kids and called it *Naomi's Road*.

WHERE HAS IT LIVED?

A more fitting question would be how did the house survive? In 2005, the owner of the house contacted the City of Vancouver about having it demolished. This sparked the formation of the Save Kogawa House Committee and a countrywide campaign to save the landmark. People from all walks of life contributed, from other writers and writing organizations to TLC, the Land Conservancy of BC. Donations were received from Canadians everywhere, including a generous donation from **feminist philanthropist** Nancy Ruth. A group of local Grade 3 and 4 students worked tirelessly to raise awareness, writing letters and appealing to the city mayor and council. They painted a banner that still hangs in the house today.

WHERE DO THE ITEMS COME FROM?

After the house was saved, Joy Kogawa donated many personal family items. Some treasured pieces, like a 1937 calendar, originally hung on the walls of the house before the war and then travelled with the family, first to the internment camp near Slocan City, then to a small sugar beet farming village called Coaldale in southern Alberta, and then home again to Vancouver. The blanket that covered Joy's mother's bed also went with the family into internment and now is home again, worn but well loved.

HOW HAS IT CHANGED?

The house Joy lived in before the Second World War later became home to many other families. They changed it in a number of ways. In the 1970s, a dining room and second bathroom were added, and original cedar shakes were covered with a stucco exterior. In the early 2000s, walls were added to make a rooming house for students. The Historic Joy Kogawa House Society has worked to restore the original finishes and floorplan and is undertaking life safety and accessibility upgrades so people of all **mobilities** can visit.

Image courtesy Ksenia Makaganova.

meet someone you admire face to face.

LIFE-SIZE CUT-OUT OF JOY KOGAWA

The cut-out was made for an exhibit called *The Party* at the Royal BC Museum in Victoria to celebrate BC150, a program of events in 2008 to celebrate 150 years since British Columbia joined Confederation.

Image courtesy Ksenia Makaganova, with original image for cut-out by Deb Martin and Todd Wong.

The Party featured 150 of the most remarkable British Columbians, past and present.

Other members of the party included actor Michael J. Fox, rodeo champ Kenny McLean, the Okanagan's Ogopogo, artist Emily Carr, and First Nations Chief Robert Sam.

The Royal BC Museum had contacted Joy Kogawa because they wanted to include a full-length picture of her for the exhibit, but Joy didn't like the photograph the museum had selected, and the pictures Joy did like weren't full length.

Todd Wong, a key player in the campaign to protect Historic Joy Kogawa House, and Deb Martin, another founding member, offered to do a photo session with Joy. The pictures turned out wonderfully and the museum was happy to select this image from the six photographs presented.

After the exhibit ended, Todd Wong donated the life-size cut-out, and it came to live at Historic Joy Kogawa House.

It's traditional for authors who live or read at Historic Joy Kogawa House to pose with the cut-out for a commemorative photograph.

JUST THE FACTS

WHAT IS IT? This is a fabric version of Joy's children's book, *Naomi's Tree*, created by a Japanese women's **fibre art** group called Nuno Ehon. The group creates fabric art books in a suburb of a city called Fukuoka known as Sue-machi.

WHAT DOES IT LOOK LIKE? The cover features a gnarled cherry tree with a twisted trunk. Its branches are covered with pink blossoms. Petals fly in the breeze as a group of children hold hands to circle the tree.

WHERE DOES IT COME FROM? The Canada–Japan Friendship Association donated the fabric book.

WHAT'S ITS STORY? Mrs. Tamako Copithorne, a Vancouver resident who had encouraged many cultural collaborations between Japan and Canada, read *Naomi's Tree* by Joy Kogawa. She presented Haruyo Handa, the leader of the Canada–Japan Friendship Association, as well as artists working as Nuno Ehon, with copies of the children's picture book. When they read it, they were all deeply moved by the story and wanted others to know about it.

Tell Me More

In the spring of 2014, Nuno Ehon decided to create *Naomi's Tree*. The artists cut small pieces from recycled fabric, including old kimonos, and **appliquéd** them onto larger pieces of cloth. The project required patience and skill, as the artists wanted the colours and illustrations to be as faithful as possible to the original book. Their goal was to meet each week to complete the project by spring of 2015. The book was finished by February 2015. It took a total of eight months.

FABRIC BOOK VERSION OF NAOMI'S TREE

WOULD YOU BELIEVE?

Nuno Ehon has been making Japanese children's books for many years. The group visits kindergartens, elementary schools, and junior high schools to read the stories and show its work.

My Turn

Think of a story you love. Choose one scene from that story and illustrate it by drawing or by using another form of art.

This fabric version of *Naomi's Tree* shows the power of Joy Kogawa's writing. Her story inspired people thousands of kilometres away to share her experiences through their art.

Images courtesy Lydia Nagai.

WHY IS *NAOMI'S TREE* IMPORTANT IN THIS AREA?

Naomi's Tree, along with Joy's other books, played a key role in teaching Canadians of all ages about the experiences of Japanese Canadians during the Second World War internment. Joy was inspired to write her first novel, *Obasan*, after reading letters written by a Japanese Canadian woman who described the hardships of internment life. Joy wanted Canadians to understand what it's like to be a victim of racism and to seek justice for Japanese Canadians who'd been displaced from their homes to rough internment camps.

JUST THE FACTS

WHAT IS IT? This is a pine desk painted white.

WHAT DOES IT LOOK LIKE? A desk inscribed with the message, "I've had this desk for years and years... hope it serves you as well as it served me...many poems, a couple of novels – goodbye desk – Love Joy Kogawa, April 20, 1996."

WHERE DOES IT COME FROM? The desk was part of a fundraiser where either it did not sell or was held back from sale by Joy.

WHAT'S ITS STORY? At this desk, Joy wrote her novel *Obasan*, which tells the story of a displaced family living through the war. The main character, Naomi, like many Japanese Canadians, endures brutal mistreatment. Through the novel, Kogawa conveys the **devastating** effects of the internment. Simply by writing this celebrated book, Joy Kogawa registers her refusal to keep quiet about the cruelty of racism.

Tell Me More

Joy was 6 years old when her family was forced by the government of Canada to move out of their Vancouver home – now known as Historic Joy Kogawa House. From there, they went straight to an internment camp in the interior of British Columbia. The family lived in a log house at the base of the mountains in an area called Brandon, north of the main street of Slocan City. A former mining town, Slocan had pre-existing buildings that were repurposed to create the internment centre. Later, those living at the camp built rudimentary shacks. In the summer these were very hot and in the winter, cold. Together, internment sites around Slocan housed nearly 5,000 internees.

Lower Mainland

› HISTORIC JOY KOGAWA HOUSE

JOY'S DESK

Image courtesy Ksenia Makaganova.

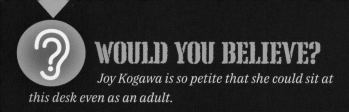

WOULD YOU BELIEVE?

Joy Kogawa is so petite that she could sit at this desk even as an adult.

My Turn

Has something happened to you that you think would make a good story? Have you ever thought of writing about it? Stories are powerful, and yours might just help someone feel less alone. Worried about having to write? No worries, there's lots of ways to share a story. Why not tell your story through drawings or a song. Both are great ways to spin a tale.

CONNECTIONS

In Dawson City, Yukon, visitors can learn about another writer, Jack London. The Jack London Museum is filled with **memorabilia**, letters, photographs, and archives from the famous American writer's life. In 1897, when Jack was 21, he moved to Dawson City, hoping to strike it rich in the Klondike Gold Rush. That didn't happen, but his adventures in Yukon would inspire his best-known books, *White Fang* and *The Call of the Wild*. In 2020, *The Call of the Wild* was made into a movie starring Harrison Ford.

 ## WHY IS THE DESK IMPORTANT IN THIS AREA?

The desk helps us understand Joy's writing life. Looking at it, we can picture her sitting there writing and rewriting. It gives us a taste of what a writer's life is like. It also shows us that Joy had to live simply and within her means.

SCIENCE WORLD

Image courtesy Science World.

JUST THE FACTS

WHERE IS IT? 1455 Quebec Street, Vancouver, BC, V6A 3Z7
(604) 443-7440
www.scienceworld.ca
Science World is located on the traditional, unceded
territory of the xʷməθkʷəy̓əm (Musqueam), S̲kwx̱wú7mesh
(Squamish), and səlilwətaɬ (Tsleil-Waututh) Peoples.

ARE PHOTOGRAPHS ALLOWED? Yes.

HOW DID IT START? In 1977, a series of hands-on science and
technology exhibits were displayed in different locations
around Vancouver. In 1982, a temporary home was found
for an Arts, Sciences and Technology Centre. After Expo '86
closed, the people of Vancouver wanted to turn the building
into a science centre and, with donations from governments,
businesses, foundations, and ordinary people like us, Science
World became a reality.

WHERE HAS IT LIVED?

Science World has always lived in this fabulous building – a
bright, shiny, geodesic dome. When Expo '86 closed, money
was raised to renovate the building, adding to the dome and
creating exhibit spaces.

WHERE DO THE ITEMS COME FROM?

Some items are designed and built by the tech team at the
centre. Some are exhibits from other centres that were
no longer needed. Still others are developed by outside
companies.

HOW HAS IT CHANGED?

Science, engineering, the arts, and technology change.
Science World changes with them. You may see some
exhibits that have been there from the beginning, but you
will also see exhibits that use state-of-the-art technology.
Old or new, there are many things to do and learn from the
permanent and temporary exhibits at Science World.

open your mind to new ways of looking at things.
SCINTILLATING GRID ILLUSION

Image courtesy Alamy.

The scintillating grid on the left is an optical illusion. Optical illusions trick our brains and eyes into seeing something that is not there.

At a specific distance away from the image, when we look around the grid, the dots flash from black to white, even though they are all white.

When you focus on one dot (it's in the centre of your field of vision), it will always be white. Dots that are not in the centre of your vision will flash from black to white. Give it a try.

See what happens if you tilt you head on a 45-degree angle. What happens if you go very close or very far away from the image?

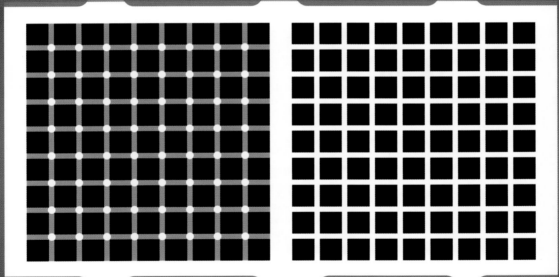

Not all people see optical illusions the same way. You could be standing next to your friend who is seeing this illusion a different way than you are.

The word "illusion" comes from the Latin *illudere*, meaning "to mock." To mock someone means to make fun of them. Can you think of a way this illusion "makes fun of us"?

The scintillating grid is closely related to the Hermann grid on the right. Ludimar Hermann first wrote about the illusion in 1870. Compare the two grids: How are they different from each other?

J.R. Bergen created the scintillating grid in 1985 – over 100 years after the Hermann grid.

JUST THE FACTS

WHAT IS IT? This is a **cast** of a *Tyrannosaurus rex*.

WHAT DOES IT LOOK LIKE? This dinosaur is just over 12 metres long and 4 metres tall. That's about six times as long as your bed and higher than two refrigerators piled on top of each other.

WHERE DOES IT COME FROM? Stan (also known as BHI 3033) was found in South Dakota in the United States. The cast of his skeleton arrived at Science World from the Black Hills Institute of Geological Research in 2009.

WHAT'S ITS STORY? Stan was discovered by, and then named after, fossil hunter Stan Sacrison. As Sacrison was searching for plants near Buffalo, South Dakota, he saw the dinosaur's pelvis (hip bone) sticking out of the side of a cliff.

Tell Me More

The *T. rex* was way too big for Sacrison to dig out himself. He needed help. That's when the Black Hills Institute of Geological Research stepped in. It took 30,000 hours and a lot of special equipment – like small earth-moving machines, picks, shovels, and even tools like those a dentist uses – to dig out the *T. rex*. Remember, the team didn't want to damage any part of him, so they were very careful. Although they couldn't find all Stan's bones (they've got 200), his skeleton was about 68 per cent complete. That makes him the fifth-most-complete *T. rex* ever found. The bones were carefully wrapped in protective material before they were moved back to the institute.

Image courtesy Science World.

Lower Mainland

> **SCIENCE WORLD**

STAN THE DINOSAUR

WOULD YOU BELIEVE?

Stan had many injuries while he was still alive. The most amazing is the hole in the back of his skull that is the exact size of a Tyrannosaurus rex's *tooth. Chances are he was attacked by another* Tyrannosaurus rex, *but he lived! Scientists know this because a thin layer of bone had grown over the hole.*

My Turn

Who do you think fossils belong to, the landowner, the people who discover them, the people who dig them up, or the country in which they are found?

Image courtesy Science World.

WHY IS STAN THE *T. REX* IMPORTANT IN THIS AREA?

The Black Hills Institute of Geological Research made molds of Stan's bones with a special silicone rubber, then made casts of the bones from a material that is a little like plastic. They were able to 3D print missing bones based on bones from other *T. rexes* that had been found. Museums and science centres around the world could buy a copy of the *T. rex* to display. And that's why you are lucky enough to see Stan today. You can compare your size to his. You can see he's a therapod – which means "beast foot" in Greek – with three toes and two legs. And you can observe Stan's 30-centimetre-long teeth. Both the front and back of each tooth is serrated. (If you think about a bread knife with its jagged edges, you'll have a good idea what Stan's teeth feel like.) Because we can see Stan, we can imagine Earth millions of years ago.

CONNECTIONS

When we study fossils, we learn about the plants and animals that lived thousands, sometimes millions, of years ago. Paleontologists – people who study fossils – know that about 56 million years ago there was a period of global warming that lasted for about 180,000 years. They can investigate how plants and animals changed over that time. They can also explore why some became extinct. With this knowledge, they can compare what happened in the past with what is happening to our climate right now and predict what might happen in the future.

WHAT IS IT? This is a reconstructed beaver lodge that was once home to a family of beavers.

WHAT DOES IT LOOK LIKE? To someone who has never seen a beaver lodge, it probably looks like some weird random pile of sticks.

WHERE DOES IT COME FROM? It came from the University of British Columbia's Malcolm Knapp Research Forest. The university offered the lodge to Science World and it said, "We'd love it!"

WHAT'S ITS STORY? A family of beavers used this lodge. For some reason – no one knows why – it was abandoned.

Lower Mainland
› SCIENCE WORLD

BEAVER LODGE

Tell Me More

In 1989, researchers at the Malcolm Knapp Research Forest noticed a beautiful beaver lodge. For many months they watched the lodge for signs of beavers but saw no activity. The beavers had left the lodge. When Science World agreed to take the lodge, they couldn't just lift it up and plunk it down on the floor. They photographed the lodge, so they knew exactly how the beavers had built it before they took it apart. Natural materials like mud and sticks have lots of things you wouldn't want crawling around Science World, like bugs and bacteria. Every stick had to be washed and vacuumed. Then a team put it back together.

Image courtesy Science World.

WOULD YOU BELIEVE?

This lodge is on the small side – between three and four metres long and one metre high. The largest lodge recorded (up until 2011) was four times this size at over 12 metres long. That's more than 12 giant steps. This huge lodge was almost five metres high, about the height of a giraffe!

Image courtesy Science World.

Beavers are a keystone species when it comes to **biodiversity**. That means when they cut down trees, build dams, turn streams into ponds, and even cause flooding, different types of plants grow and insects, fish, birds, turtles, and other wildlife find new habitat.

My Turn

How many reasons can you think of for why beavers build the entrances and exits to their lodges underwater?

⭐ WHY IS THE BEAVER LODGE IMPORTANT IN THIS AREA?

Beavers build their lodges one stick at a time using mud to glue the sticks together. They are excellent swimmers, so the entrances and exits to their houses are underwater. When the team rebuilt the lodge in Science World, they thought it looked cool, but they wondered how visitors would learn about the way beaver lodges fit into the community and into the ecosystem. They opened up a part of the lodge so you can crawl inside and see the lodge the way a beaver does. (And you don't even have to get wet!) Then they added a layer of Plexiglas where the lake level would be so you can understand where the lodge sits in the water and what plants and birds share the same ecosystem. One day they hope to film the local False Creek beavers. Then you'll be able to see how beavers live in these lodges in their natural environment.

HIPPO LEVER

WHAT IS IT? This is an exhibit that teaches about the power of levers.

WHAT DOES IT LOOK LIKE? At one end a hippo sits in a box. A harness attaches her to a long pole that is marked off in metres and feet. The pole rests on a large triangle that acts as a fulcrum (or support). A rope hangs from the bar and can be moved closer or father away from the hippo.

WHERE DOES IT COME FROM? This lever has been exhibited at Science World since the early 1990s. The hippo was sculpted for Science World and added to the lever in 2003. How old does that make the hippo?

WHAT'S ITS STORY? Millions of people have jumped on, hung from, and played on the hippo lever. But no one can sit on the hippo, thank you very much.

Tell Me More

Could you lift a grand piano all by yourself? Probably not, unless you knew about levers. A lever is an example of a simple machine, something that makes hard work easier. The hippo lever can help you lift a 150-kilogram hippo – that's like lifting a grand piano. A lever is a long bar that is balanced on something underneath. That something is called a fulcrum. Think about a teeter-totter. Right in the middle of the teeter-totter is a support. When there are two people on the teeter-totter, one can lift the other into the air quite easily.

Image courtesy Science World.

? WOULD YOU BELIEVE?

Originally, the lever lifted a pile of plate weights like you might see in a gym on the end of a barbell. That's ok, but not nearly as fun as lifting a hippo.

Image courtesy Science World.

The hippo lever is a favourite with visitors young and old. Adults who came to Science World as children bring their children to try to lift the hippo. Not only do they want their kids to try it, they still want to give it a go. No doubt, when those children grow up, they will bring their own kids. Seeing science in action never seems to get old.

My Turn

The hippo lever is one kind of lever. Scissors are the same kind of lever. Can you explain how scissors are like the hippo lever?

★ WHY IS THE HIPPO LEVER IMPORTANT IN THIS AREA?

The hippo lever is an example of learning through play. By moving the rope to different parts of the pole, you can discover where you can easily lift the hippo and where it gets really hard (and then impossible). If you move the rope farther away from the fulcrum and pull on the rope, it is easy to lift the hippo. It takes less effort to lift the load. The closer you slide the rope toward the fulcrum, the more effort it will take to lift the hippo. Eventually, you'll have to have help. Have you ever been on a teeter-totter with someone heavier than you? Moving to the very end of the plank (away from the fulcrum) probably helped you lift that extra weight more easily. But if the other person (the load) is too heavy, no matter how much effort you make, you won't be able to lift your partner.

JUST THE FACTS

WHAT IS IT? This is a camera and projector that make invisible light visible.

WHAT DOES IT LOOK LIKE? It's a blank wall, but when you stand in front of the camera mounted at the top, your body is projected in infrared light.

WHERE DOES IT COME FROM? A company, FLIR, developed the software, and Science World mounted a projector that made the image cover the wall.

WHAT'S ITS STORY? Like a lot of technology, much of the "magic" is hidden. Your body is always giving off invisible infrared light. The camera detects that light, and the software re-colours the light so you can see it in colours your eyes can understand. Warm parts of your body look white and yellow and colder ones look blue or green.

Tell Me More

A German-born, British **astronomer** named Sir Frederick William Herschel discovered infrared light in 1800, long before Confederation. He used a **prism** to break white light into seven colours. He then measured the temperature of each colour with a thermometer. As he moved from violet to red, he found that each colour increased the temperature reading on the thermometer. Violet was the coolest and red the warmest. Herschel then measured the temperature of the space just next to the red and found it was even hotter. He didn't name it infrared, but that's what it was.

Image courtesy Science World.

INFRARED CAMERA

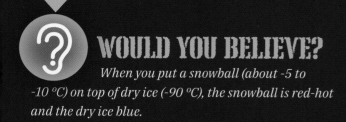

WOULD YOU BELIEVE?

When you put a snowball (about -5 to -10 °C) on top of dry ice (-90 °C), the snowball is red-hot and the dry ice blue.

What can you learn about ultraviolet light – the light that's above or beyond violet? Are there any animals that can see ultraviolet light?

You might have heard of night vision goggles that let you see in the dark. That's one use of infrared technology. During the winter, we can use infrared cameras to see how much heat our windows are letting out, or how much cold they are letting in. The infrared wall at Science World helps you understand a bit more about infrared light and your own body heat.

WHY IS THE INFRARED CAMERA IMPORTANT IN THIS AREA?

All objects give off heat in the form of infrared radiation. Of course, hot things like burners on stoves give off heat, but even the coldest things you can think of give off heat. Infrared cameras sense differences in temperature and create images based on this information. They use colours to show us whether something is hot or cold – bright colours like red, orange, yellow, and white for parts that are hotter, and purple, dark blue, and black for parts that are cooler. So when you are seeing yourself projected on the wall in infrared light, your hands may be colder than your armpits. They may be blue, while your underarms may be yellow. This shows us something pretty cool: people actually glow in the dark. Some animals like bees, butterflies, and mosquitos can see infrared light. To a mosquito, in the dark we look like a candle!

MISSION MUSEUM

JUST THE FACTS

WHERE IS IT? 33201 2nd Avenue, Mission, BC, V2V 4L1
(604) 826-1011
https://missionmuseum.com
Mission's first inhabitants were the Stó:lō People, including
Leq'á:mel, Semá:th, Kwantlen, Sq'éwlets, Máthexwi, and
Katzie First Nations.

ARE PHOTOGRAPHS ALLOWED? Yes, photographs are
encouraged at the museum. But, please, no flash!

HOW DID IT START? The museum opened on March 22, 1972,
in a **prefabricated** Bank of Commerce building constructed
in 1907. This was thanks to the efforts of the newly formed
Mission District Historical Society, started by the former
mayor of Mission, Ethel Ogle, its founding president. In 1969,
the society started meeting regularly "to plan for a museum,
should the opportunity arrive." It had also begun collecting
items of historical value to the community and storing them at
Ogle's home.

WHERE HAS IT LIVED?

Mission Museum has always been located at 33201 2nd
Avenue, but the building itself has done its fair share of
travelling. In 1907, it was located on 1st Avenue, where it
was the Bank of Commerce. Then, in the mid-1940s, the
bank replaced it with a new brick structure, so the museum
building was moved up one block to its current address.
From around 1947 to 1970, it was home to Mission's public
library until a new facility was constructed farther down
the block.

WHERE DO THE ITEMS COME FROM?

Mission's citizens, people connected to the city, community
groups, businesses, and the City of Mission itself donate
the artifacts. Sometimes artifacts arrive via transfer from
the museum's sister branch, the Mission Community
Archives. Along with the artifacts gathered by the founding
historical society, the **bedrock** of the museum's collection
came from Anthony Taulbut, who was an avid collector,
historian, explorer, and pioneer. He was born in Fareham,
Hampshire, England, in 1874, and travelled the world
during his time in the Royal Navy. After his service, he
immigrated to Canada with his wife in 1908. They arrived
in Mission with 52 huge boxes full of artifacts in tow. While
in Mission, he sold real estate, served as a school board
secretary, delivered the post, and ran a museum out of his
house. In 1972, members of his family began donating his
collection to the Mission Museum.

HOW HAS IT CHANGED?

Originally, the museum building housed both the artifact
and archival collection, then in 1989 a purpose-built
archival storage room was built as a separate branch. The
museum was completely volunteer-run until 1994, when
the society received funding from the District of Mission
(now the City of Mission) to hire the community's first paid
curator and archivist.

Images courtesy Mission Museum staff.

Imagine what it's like to be a soapbox derby driver.
1969 SOAPBOX DERBY CHAMPION JACKET AND COMPETITOR'S HELMET

After the hardships of the Second World War, Mission residents needed a celebration, so the board of trade rallied together with local businessmen to start the Strawberry Festival.

Most soapbox derby cars took two to three months to build.

By 1950, the derby was a province-wide contest attracting big name sponsors. The newspaper *The Province* gave the event full-page publicity, praising Mission's strong community spirit.

The first festival in 1946 was held on Main Street, from Grand Street to Horne Street. It was a huge success.

In 1956, the derby attracted 20,000 visitors to Mission. Two years later, it had over 200 contestants representing over 40 different communities.

Boys ages 11 to 16 could enter the soapbox derby. Their cars had to be built to strict specifications.

The derby was cancelled in 1974, but in 1999 it started again under the sponsorship of the Mission & District Lions Club. It has taken place annually ever since.

The boys entering the contest could not receive any help other than advice.

JUST THE FACTS

WHAT IS IT? This is a travelling trunk that once belonged to Bunjiro Sakon, a Japanese Canadian pioneer and brilliant **agriculturalist** in Mission, BC. He arrived with it when he came to Canada from Japan in 1899.

WHAT DOES IT LOOK LIKE? Imagine a large brown leather suitcase too big to fit under your seat or in the overhead storage of a plane. If it were full, you'd probably have to drag it wherever you were going.

WHERE DOES IT COME FROM? Bunjiro's granddaughter donated the trunk. He used the trunk on his journey by railway car to Alberta, where he farmed sugar beets through the Second World War during his internment.

WHAT'S ITS STORY? Bunjiro was an Issei, a first-generation Japanese immigrant, who farmed in Mission from 1904 to 1942. There were over 100 Japanese families in the area. In 1916, the Japanese farmers established the Nokkai, a farming co-op to launch their produce into the Canadian market, which could be hard for non-white immigrants. The co-op built a hall for meetings and social gatherings. More than just an agricultural business, the Nokkai represented the Issei community, providing a link to the rest of Mission.

Lower Mainland
› MISSION MUSEUM
BUNJIRO SAKON'S TRUNK

Tell Me More

The Issei soon established themselves as very hard-working and were admired in Mission for transforming the thick brush on the hills into fertile farmland. They grew mostly berries and shipped their crops internationally. Bunjiro Sakon bred two popular crops, a hothouse rhubarb designed to thrive inside a greenhouse, and an autumn strawberry, which could fruit in colder weather. These crops extended the growing season, allowing farmers to profit from the produce longer. The Nokkai would take turns growing certain crops so the market wouldn't become flooded, ensuring everyone would make a decent living. Soon they became such a force in the area that non-Japanese farmers wanted to join. As a result, the **Pacific Cooperative Union** (or PCU) was formed in 1932.

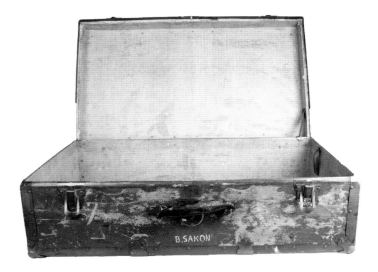

WOULD YOU BELIEVE?

Just like when you take turns while playing games, the Nokkai farmers took turns growing certain popular crops. This cooperation meant every family had a chance to make a good living.

My Turn

What do you do when you feel overwhelmed? Do you go somewhere or do something? What's your favourite form of comfort? The writers of this book are very fond of chocolate when they're feeling blue.

CONNECTIONS

David Suzuki, the well-known TV broadcaster, scientist, and environmental activist, is a third-generation Japanese Canadian. When he was very young, his parents owned a dry cleaning shop in Vancouver, but after the Second World War broke out, his family was forced into internment in Slocan, BC. David was only 5 years old. Their new home in an old hotel was run down and very dingy. At the camp, other kids teased David because he didn't speak Japanese.

In order to survive this difficult period, David escaped to the woods and learned how to fish. Maybe this is one of the reasons why he's such an advocate for the environment. After the war, his family moved to Leamington, Ontario. This further fuelled his interest in the natural world as he explored the nearby swamps. For him, areas like these were thrilling and mysterious because of the variety of plant and animal life.

WHY IS BUNJIRO SAKON'S TRUNK IMPORTANT IN THIS AREA?

The trunk serves as a reminder of the two important journeys Bunjiro took in his life, one by choice, the other by force. On December 7, 1941, everything changed for Bunjiro and other Issei when Japan entered the Second World War, attacking the US military base at **Pearl Harbor**, leading both Canada and the US to declare war on Japan. Overnight, Japanese Canadians were added to the list of potential enemy aliens. Suddenly regarded as spies, calls began from various groups seeking **mass deportation** of the Japanese, regardless of citizenship. Although Mission's Japanese Canadian residents had supported the war effort by buying the most war bonds prior to Japan's attack, they were still viewed by some as potential enemies. Mission's Japanese Canadian residents were given an extension to allow time to plant their crops, but in April 1942 residents were given their orders to go and give up all financial assets to a **Custodian of Enemy Property** for "safekeeping."

JUST THE FACTS

WHAT IS IT? This is a Stó:lō netting needle.

WHAT DOES IT LOOK LIKE? The hand-carved needle is made with cedar, a wood that is strong, lightweight, and straight-grained. It's the ideal material for skilled makers to carve other fishing instruments such as canoes, paddles, hooks, spears, ropes, and floats.

WHERE DOES IT COME FROM? The needle is part of the museum's Stó:lō exhibit developed in co-operation with the Stó:lō Tribal Council, **archeologist** Gordon Mohs, and the Coqualeetza Cultural Education Centre in Chilliwack, which donated several Stó:lō songs. The Mission Friendship Centre donated the needle in 1978.

WHAT'S ITS STORY? The tool was used to make and mend cedar fishing nets and is wound with cedar twine. The twine is tied to the base of the "tongue" in the eye of the needle and wound around the pronged end and back up to either side of the tongue. The needle helps the user to connect the twine in a series of loops and knots.

Lower Mainland

› **MISSION MUSEUM**

NETTING NEEDLE

Tell Me More

Stó:lō means "People of the River" as they relied on the Fraser River and its **tributaries** for their way of life. Their villages were mostly concentrated on the waterway. During certain seasons, Stó:lō families would travel to different dwellings situated by prime fishing or gathering spots. Their most important food source was salmon. A staple food in the diet year-round, it was considered to be the descendants of a Stó:lō ancestor who had been transformed into the fish by the Great Creator so the people would never go hungry. As such, the salmon is prized and placed in high respect during ceremonies and spiritual gatherings. This sort of interconnectedness between people and the natural world is still a major part of Stó:lō spirituality. *Shxwelí,* or life force, connects all living things with the earth, as well as connecting the present with the generations past and future.

WOULD YOU BELIEVE?

Many months in the Stó:lō calendar are named for important points in the fishing season. For example, Temtheqi, the 11th month, is sockeye salmon time.

My Turn

The Stó:lō People take their name for the river that is such a meaningful part of their lives. If you could name yourself after a major part of your life, what would your name be?

The Stó:lō **econom**y was based on a **reciprocal** exchange program called the *t'leaxet*, or Potlatch, where villages would gift each other delicacies and supplies needed for both survival and pleasure. The Stó:lō are not alone in this. Many **cultures** around the world have **rituals** that include gift giving connected to survival. In Japan, the celebration Shichi-Go-San, which means Seven-Five-Three, is celebrated on November 15 and dedicated to children ages 7, 5, and 3, who are given a gift of red and white candies called Chitose by the priest at the local shrine. The candy symbolizes longevity and good health. Shichi-Go-San began hundreds and hundreds of years ago, when children often died before their third, fifth, and seventh birthdays. During this time, parents showed gratitude to the gods for their children. It was believed that until children reached the age of 7, they belonged to the gods.

⭐ WHY IS THE NETTING NEEDLE IMPORTANT IN THIS AREA?

Although archeologists place the arrival of the Stó:lō about 4,000 to 10,000 years ago, the Stó:lō themselves believe they have been here for time immemorial. According to Creation Stories, the Stó:lō are descended from the Sky People and the Earth People, and were given their territory, or Solh Temexw, by the Great Creator. Oral histories surrounding the Great Creator and the beginning of the world have been passed down through centuries of generations until the present day.

BRITANNIA SHIPYARDS NATIONAL HISTORIC SITE

JUST THE FACTS

WHERE IS IT? 5180 Westwater Drive, Richmond, BC, V7E 6P3
(604) 238-8050
http://britanniashipyards.ca/
Hən̓q̓əmin̓əm̓-speaking people have lived and harvested these lands and waters for thousands of years, including the Musqueam, Stó:lō Treaty Nation, and Tsawwassen Nation.

ARE PHOTOGRAPHS ALLOWED? Visitors are welcome to take interior photos provided no equipment is set up and the pathways are not blocked for others.

HOW DID IT START? The site is named after the largest building on the property, the Britannia Shipyard. Built as a salmon cannery in 1889, it became a shipyard in 1918 and was later owned by the Canadian Fishing Company and the BC Packers. In 1991, it was made a historic site of **national significance** because of its **representation** of the fishing and boatbuilding industries in Steveston, the **diverse** people, and the extraordinary river that supported these industries from their beginnings to the present. It opened to the public in 1995.

Images courtesy City of Richmond.

WHERE HAS IT LIVED?

The majority of the buildings are original to this site. A few were relocated from nearby Garry Point or as far away as Knight Inlet. All the buildings help to tell the story of west coast boatbuilding heritage.

WHERE DO THE ITEMS COME FROM?

The artifacts on display are part of the City of Richmond's collection. These objects tell the story of the growth of the area, as well as its history and culture. The interactive displays, touchable objects, and props are all true to the period and chosen to give visitors an up-close experience.

HOW HAS IT CHANGED?

Over the years, new hands-on experiences and heritage activities were added to make the site more accessible and **inclusive** for everyone. Some of the activities reflect the **multicultural** backgrounds of the people who used to live and work here, including **origami** in the Murakami House, Chinese calligraphy and **tangrams** in the Chinese Bunkhouse, and lawn games on the outdoor festival field. In the future, there are plans for more historic buildings to be restored and opened to the public, including the First Nations Bunkhouse, Japanese Duplex, and Phoenix Net Loft, to share the tales of the people who lived and worked here.

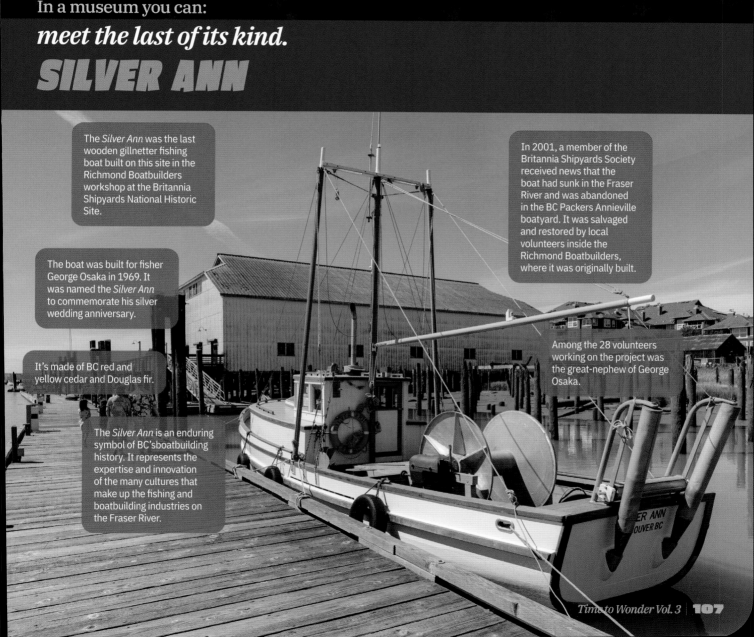

In a museum you can:

meet the last of its kind.

SILVER ANN

The *Silver Ann* was the last wooden gillnetter fishing boat built on this site in the Richmond Boatbuilders workshop at the Britannia Shipyards National Historic Site.

In 2001, a member of the Britannia Shipyards Society received news that the boat had sunk in the Fraser River and was abandoned in the BC Packers Annieville boatyard. It was salvaged and restored by local volunteers inside the Richmond Boatbuilders, where it was originally built.

The boat was built for fisher George Osaka in 1969. It was named the *Silver Ann* to commemorate his silver wedding anniversary.

Among the 28 volunteers working on the project was the great-nephew of George Osaka.

It's made of BC red and yellow cedar and Douglas fir.

The *Silver Ann* is an enduring symbol of BC's boatbuilding history. It represents the expertise and innovation of the many cultures that make up the fishing and boatbuilding industries on the Fraser River.

JUST THE FACTS

WHAT IS IT? This is a reconstruction of the traditional Japanese wooden bathtub and bathing area built by Otokichi Murakami, a Japanese carpenter and boatbuilder. He lived in this house with his wife, Asayo, and their ten children. His workshop was next door.

WHAT DOES IT LOOK LIKE? The *ofuroba* was used in Japan before the change to more Western-style bathrooms. Many of the Murakami children remembered being encouraged into the bath by their parents with floating pieces of watermelon!

WHERE DOES IT COME FROM? The bathroom was designed for the space. The Murakami children helped by sharing their drawings and memories.

WHAT'S ITS STORY? The family lived here from 1929 to 1942, until they were forcibly uprooted along with more than 23,000 Japanese Canadian people from the west coast because of the **War Measures Act**.

› BRITANNIA SHIPYARDS NATIONAL HISTORIC SITE

MURAKAMI HOUSE OFUROBA (BATHING ROOM)

Tell Me More

The Murakami family ended up on a sugar beet farm in Letellier, Manitoba. The work there was hard and very badly paid. Workers only made 50 cents an hour. After the war, the family joined the couple's oldest daughter and her husband on a potato farm in Alberta.

Asayo went on to outlive Otokichi by 27 years. When she died at 104, she left behind 9 children, 21 grandchildren, 57 great-grandchildren, and 5 great-great-grandchildren. Her granddaughter, Linda Ohama, made a documentary about her called *Obachan's Garden*. This focused on a secret Asayo kept until she turned 100: the story of the two daughters she was forced to give up in Japan.

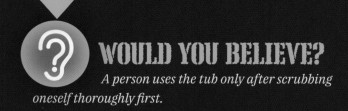

WOULD YOU BELIEVE?

A person uses the tub only after scrubbing oneself thoroughly first.

My Turn

To learn more about the lives of Japanese Canadians during the Second World War, look for these books at your library: *Stealing Home*, a graphic novel by J. Torres and David Namisato; *Dear Canada: Torn Apart: The Internment Diary of Mary Kobayashi, Vancouver, British Columbia, 1941* by Susan Aihoshi; *Flags* by Maxine Trottier; and *Naomi's Tree* by Joy Kogawa, who is featured in this book.

CONNECTIONS

In Finland, saunas are a big part of life. In case you don't know, a sauna is a small wooden room that uses dry heat to make people sweat. It looks a little like the ofuroba and there are some similar customs. For example, before going into the sauna, people shower. Temperatures can be as high as 212 degrees Fahrenheit. The wood-burning stove heats a tray of rocks and people put water on the stones to make the air steamy. The steam makes people sweat. Once people get very hot inside the sauna, they cool down by jumping in freezing cold water or snow. The oldest saunas in Finland date back several thousands of years. The first saunas were caves dug into the slopes of hills. In Finland, saunas are not only considered good for the body but good for one's mental health as well.

WHY IS THE OFUROBA IMPORTANT IN THIS AREA?

Steveston was once home to a large community of Japanese Canadians. They worked in the fishing, canning, and boatbuilding industries. In 1942, when the Canadian government forced them to leave, almost two-thirds of the population was of Japanese **descen**t. This ofuroba represents the sense of "home" crafted by the skilled workers who came to this place to build a life, only to have it snatched away.

JUST THE FACTS

WHAT IS IT? Built in 1915, this is the last-surviving Chinese bunkhouse on Canada's west coast. It was used to house up to 100 Chinese Canadian workers at the Glendale Cannery in Knight Inlet, BC. It was built in 1917 by the ABC Packing Company.

WHAT DOES IT LOOK LIKE? The bunkhouse is a 2,000-square-foot, two-storey timber building. The upstairs sleeping area is filled with roughly made, narrow bunk beds and trunks where people may have stored their belongings.

WHERE DOES IT COME FROM? The bunkhouse was floated down from Knight Inlet by barge. It was donated to the City of Richmond in 1992.

WHAT'S ITS STORY? The bunkhouse is used to show the conditions in which large numbers of cannery workers lived. Imagine living in this space with over a hundred people. It would be very cramped and loud – even if people did their very best to be quiet. The bunkhouse tells us of the important role Chinese Canadians held in the fishing and canning industries in the late 1800s to early 1900s.

› BRITANNIA SHIPYARDS NATIONAL HISTORIC SITE

CHINESE BUNKHOUSE

Tell Me More

These hard-working people had a lot to deal with when they came to Canada, such as the loneliness of leaving one's home and discrimination. Even though they helped greatly in the formation of Canada, when they first arrived, the European Canadians treated them very badly. For many years an expensive **head tax** restricted Chinese immigration to Canada. The Chinese were the only ethnic group made to pay this tax. This made bringing a wife or elderly parents to Canada very costly. So mostly they lived as bachelors in Canada.

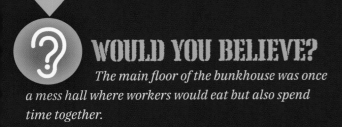

WOULD YOU BELIEVE?

The main floor of the bunkhouse was once a mess hall where workers would eat but also spend time together.

You can now learn even more about Chinese Canadian history. The first Chinese Canadian museum was founded in March 2020. It's located in the historic Wing Sang Building, the oldest building in Vancouver's Chinatown. Learn how you can visit it here: https://www.chinesecanadianmuseum.ca/about-ccm/#.

In 1999, Adrienne Clarkson became the 26th Governor General of Canada. She was the second woman to hold the position, the first without a political or military background, and, as a Chinese Canadian, the first visible minority. As the Governor General, it was her duty to represent Queen Elizabeth II in Canada. Adrienne was born in Hong Kong, China, and came to Canada to escape the Japanese occupation of that city. Her family was granted special permission to move to Canada, despite the Chinese Immigration Act, as her dad had Canadian connections through his work. When her family arrived in Ottawa as refugees, they only had one suitcase each and nothing else. Still, Adrienne recalls her experiences growing up as a refugee and immigrant as positive, even though the government policies at the time were very anti-Chinese. She says that individuals were very kind to her family.

WHY IS THE BUNKHOUSE IMPORTANT IN THIS AREA?

As the last-surviving bunkhouse on the west coast, it serves as a physical reminder of the hard lives and work of the Chinese Canadian workers. Without these workers, the fishing and canning industries would not have been as successful in their **heyday.** The City of Richmond has a large multicultural community and it's important to share the histories of all the peoples that are part of the local heritage.

MUSEUM OF SURREY

JUST THE FACTS

WHERE IS IT? 17710 – 56A Avenue, Surrey, BC, V3S 5H8
(604) 592-6956
www.surrey.ca/museum
Surrey is situated on the unceded territories of the se'mya'me (Semiahmoo), q̓ʷɑ:n̓ƛ̓ən̓ (Kwantlen), and q̓icəy̓ (Katzie) Nations.

ARE PHOTOGRAPHS ALLOWED? Yes, but no flash in the galleries, please.

HOW DID IT START? The museum opened in 1938. It began when Claude Harvey, a municipal engineer and collector of local artifacts, suggested to council that the 1881 Town Hall, the City of Surrey's first city hall, could be moved to the Cloverdale Fairgrounds and used as a museum. Today, the museum sees 100,000 visitors a year, making it the most popular municipal museum in western Canada!

WHERE HAS IT LIVED?

In 1958, the museum expanded with a structure built around the 1881 Town Hall. It was named the Surrey Centennial Museum. Later, in the 1970s, it was further expanded and renamed the Surrey Museum & Archives. In 2005, a new museum was built on the present site and further expanded in 2018 to become Museum of Surrey. Today, the 1881 Town Hall sits on the Heritage Campus with Museum of Surrey, along with two other heritage buildings: Anniedale School, built in 1891, and Anderson Cabin, Surrey's oldest settler building, built in 1872. The campus also includes Surrey Archives, Cloverdale Library, and Veterans Square.

WHERE DO THE ITEMS COME FROM?

The focus of the museum is to be welcoming, accessible, and inclusive. Staff work hard to ensure all Surrey communities are represented in exhibits, programs, and special events. Artifacts in the Surrey Stories Gallery come from Surrey residents and tell the stories of those who live in the area. There are belongings from Semiahmoo, Kwantlen, and Katzie First Nations and settlers from around the world, including recent immigrants who now call Surrey home.

HOW HAS IT CHANGED?

In 2018, the museum was renamed Museum of Surrey and expanded to include the TD Explore Zone, an interactive gallery for kids exploring **sustainability**, the Feature Gallery, which showcases exhibits about the community and the world we live in, and the Indigenous Hall, a gallery dedicated to telling the stories of Indigenous communities across the province. The exhibits in the Feature Gallery and Indigenous Hall change at least two times per year. In addition, the Surrey Stories Gallery, the main history gallery, includes a space for the Surrey community to tell its stories called Community Treasures, which changes three times per year.

In a museum you can:

remember a queen.

JACQUARD WEAVING OF QUEEN ELIZABETH II

It took more than six months to complete, and only 500 copies of the design were ever made. This is copy number 427.

This is a woven copy in silk of Pietro Annigoni's 1955 portrait of Queen Elizabeth II.

After the 500 copies were finished, the weaving pattern cards were destroyed.

The piece was made to celebrate the Queen's silver jubilee in 1977, marking the 25 years she had been on the throne.

The company Cartwright & Sheldon wove it, working in a place called Paradise Mill in Macclesfield, England. Today, Paradise Mill is a museum.

Courtesy Museum Textile Studio.

JUST THE FACTS

WHAT IS IT? This is a petroglyph, which is a stone with a carved image made using stone tools.

WHAT DOES IT LOOK LIKE? It is a dark black, round stone with an image of a face and **radiating** lines carved on the front. Don Welsh, a historian and archeologist working with the Semiahmoo First Nation, describes it as a sunburst.

WHERE DOES IT COME FROM? The petroglyph dates to about 1,500 years ago; that's like a bazillion-trillion great-great-grandparents ago. Surrey resident Canon Holdom found the petroglyph on the beach in 1957. It weighs 227 kilograms. That's about half the weight of an average horse. The Surrey School Board eventually moved the stone from the beach to the location of Surrey's first schoolhouse in the Cloverdale area of the city. It was transferred to the Surrey Museum (now called the Museum of Surrey) shortly thereafter.

WHAT'S ITS STORY? Semiahmoo Chief Harley Chappell describes it as follows: "This stone, referred to as a 'he,' is a protector. When he was on the shore, he protected the people from incoming raids from the north." Don Welsh believes it may have been made by young men on spiritual training **quests** to mark a significant tribal location.

Lower Mainland
› MUSEUM OF SURREY
SEMIAHMOO PETROGLYPH

Courtesy City of Surrey Heritage Services (1962.1027.0001).

Tell Me More

The land now known as Surrey is located on the unceded territories of the Semiahmoo, Kwantlen, and Katzie Peoples who have ancient and ongoing ties to the land. This petroglyph was found on a beach on Semiahmoo territory, in Crescent Beach. Archeological findings show the area has been continuously populated since at least 3000 BCE. The Semiahmoo First Nation's traditional territory spans from south of the United States–Canada border and north of the Fraser River in Canada. The Semiahmoo continue to be a vibrant part of Surrey's community. They take pride in being from the land, and they take great care to ensure the protection of the land, water, animals, and people according to cultural teachings.

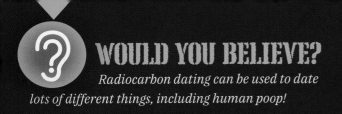

WOULD YOU BELIEVE?

Radiocarbon dating can be used to date lots of different things, including human poop!

My Turn

Interested in learning more about radiocarbon dating? There are some great chemistry videos on YouTube for kids. One of our favourites is "How Carbon Dating Works" by *BrainStuff – HowStuffWorks* (https://www.youtube.com/watch?v=Kcuz1JiMk9k). We highly recommend it.

When archeologists don't know how old a petroglyph is, they use something called radiocarbon dating. This is a process of measuring the age of carbon-bearing materials up to 60,000 years old. What is carbon? Carbon is made from stars and is the most magical element on our planet. Some forms of carbon you may be familiar with are soot, charcoal, and diamonds.

Willard Libby first developed radiocarbon dating in the late 1940s at the University of Chicago. It's an important tool for anyone studying the past. But it's not perfect. Radiocarbon dating is very expensive and not always 100 per cent reliable.

WHY IS THE PETROGLYPH IMPORTANT IN THIS AREA?

The petroglyph is currently on display in the museum's Indigenous Hall. This is a space of gathering, storytelling, and exhibition that is voiced completely by the communities it represents: Katzie First Nation, Kwantlen First Nation, and Semiahmoo First Nation. It's a dynamic and active space intended to educate.

Lower Mainland

> **MUSEUM OF SURREY**

JACQUARD LOOM

WHAT IS IT? This is a large **mechanical** loom owned and used by Honey Hooser. This type of loom uses a **punched card system** to create textiles with complex patterns woven into the fabric such as brocade, which has a raised pattern, damask, which features a reversible pattern, and *matelassé*, a woven material that looks like it's quilted or padded.

WHAT DOES IT LOOK LIKE? Imagine a large wooden frame about the size of a queen-size bed with metal brackets to keep it in place. From the top of the frame hangs a twisted hank of yarn.

WHERE DOES IT COME FROM? Honey's son Doug donated it to the museum in 1984. It's still used today by staff and volunteers in the museum's textile studio.

WHAT'S ITS STORY? In the 1960s and '70s, Honey and her husband George were a big part of the weaving community in Surrey.

Courtesy City of Surrey Heritage Services (HWC161).

Tell Me More

George built the loom's wooden frame, but the mechanical part of the loom was manufactured in England and purchased in 1953. This loom's system is believed to have played an important role in the history of **computing hardware**, as well as being inspirational in the development of **computer programming** and **data entry**. Before the invention of this loom, complicated patterns were added to the fabric after it was woven. In her career as a weaver, Honey created many beautiful things. Perhaps her biggest achievement was weaving a gift for Queen Elizabeth II to celebrate the birth of Princess Anne. One of her handwoven skirts was included in a set of baby clothes made for the princess.

WOULD YOU BELIEVE?

The Jacquard loom was the first machine to use punch cards to perform a job. This is why it's considered a forerunner to our modern-day computer.

My Turn

Here's a simple weaving project:

1. Gather together a paper plate, wool, scissors, and a plastic needle.

2. Cut ten slits evenly around the edge of the plate.

3. Run a piece of wool lengthwise from the top slit to the bottom slit. Move clockwise, weaving the wool back and forth across the plate.

4. Thread the plastic needle with wool.

5. Starting at the centre of the plate, use your needle to go over, under, and around the lengthwise wool.

6. Once your project is finished, cut the wool from the plate and tie up the ends.

CONNECTIONS

In 1804, when French weaver and merchant Joseph-Marie Jacquard invented the Jacquard loom, he completely changed the way patterned cloth could be woven. His design, built on an invention by Jacques de Vaucanson, made it possible for unskilled labourers to make patterns usually woven by a master weaver and assistant. Before this invention, the weaver's assistant, known as a "draw boy," sat on top of the loom, raising and lowering the length-wise threads to make the patterns in the cloth. As you can imagine, this was slow. Thanks to Jacquard, the process became faster, which meant the cost of patterned cloth became less expensive as it could be mass produced and available to more people. The secret to the machine's speed? Cards with small holes punched in them. These were the instructions for the pattern.

WHY IS THE LOOM IMPORTANT IN THIS AREA?

Honey was a **mentor** to many would-be weavers during her artistic career. She taught people from all walks of life and people with **disabilities**, including soldiers who'd been hurt in the Second World War. Today, her legacy continues in the form of a scholarship for high school students or a person with disabilities with a passion in arts and crafts.

JUST THE FACTS

WHAT IS IT? This is a horse-drawn buggy used by Freda Gunst. The buggy was likely made around 1899, but Freda began driving it in 1960.

WHAT DOES IT LOOK LIKE? It looks as if it belongs in a movie set in the Old West, like the animated movie *Spirit*.

WHERE DOES IT COME FROM? Freda donated it to the Museum of Surrey in 2003. It can be seen in the Celebrations Section of the Surrey Stories Gallery. Two other artifacts belonging to Freda are in the collection: riding chaps embroidered with her name, and a decorative horse bit.

WHAT'S ITS STORY? Freda Gunst was born in 1913 and grew up on a farm just outside Cloverdale. When she was young, she would ride her horse into town. Freda went all around Surrey and beyond in this buggy, pulled by her team of Arabian horses: Silver, Copper, and Patra. Can you imagine what it would be like to have your own team of horses?

Tell Me More

Freda rode in parades, horse shows, and in the 75th birthday celebration of Chief Dan George. Chief Dan George was awarded the **Order of Canada** as a respected Tsleil-Waututh actor, musician, poet, and author. Freda was often asked to transport famous people to events. She drove the politician Alex Fraser and his wife Gertrude to the opening of the Alex Fraser Bridge in Greater Vancouver, which was named in his honour.

Lower Mainland
› MUSEUM OF SURREY

FREDA GUNST'S BUGGY

My Turn

Are you crazy about horses? Check out EquiMania! on the Horse Portal on the University of Guelph's website (http://www.equimania.ca). It's got fabulous activities like horse-themed crosswords and match games and lots of fun facts about horses. You'll learn everything you need to know about these amazing creatures.

CONNECTIONS

When Freda passed away in 2010, her family asked people to donate to the Valley Therapeutic Equestrian Association. It offers **therapeutic** riding, a health treatment that uses riding to help people with a wide range of disabilities. Lis Hartel, a Danish national hero, inspired the therapy. Lis was born in 1921 and was a horse lover from childhood. She did very well in competitions. When she grew up, she married a horse lover like herself. Sadly, when she was pregnant with her second child, she got **polio**. At first, she was completely paralyzed, but her mother and husband helped her train to ride again. Before her illness, Lis was an Olympic prospect. She was determined to be one again. Eventually, she became the first woman to ride for an Olympic equestrian team and the first female medalist, despite being paralyzed from the knees down. Lis considered her best work to be opening the first therapeutic riding centre in Europe.

WHY IS THE BUGGY IMPORTANT IN THIS AREA?

Freda created the Fraser Valley Jr. Horsemen Club and was a member of several other **equestrian** associations. In 2003, she won the Horse Council of BC's Horse Person of the Year trophy – a big honour. This special woman helped to shape Surrey's equestrian community.

JUST THE FACTS

WHAT IS IT? This basket and these hand-carved trays were used for picking strawberries with their **hulls** whole. It was important that the berries looked good, as they were sold fresh.

WHAT DOES IT LOOK LIKE? The trays look very similar to the green paper ones we use today. The basket looks like it might be heavy to carry around all day.

WHERE DOES IT COME FROM? These items came from the Ota family farm and were donated by Ray Ota. His father used the trays and basket.

WHAT'S ITS STORY? Ray's parents, Yoshie Ota and Unezo Ota, the original owners of the Ota family farm, immigrated to Canada in 1923. Twelve years later, their son Meizui Rey (Ray) was born. The family had a farm in Langley, but they never even got to harvest their first crop. After Canada declared war on Japan during the Second World War, the Ota family, along with all lower mainland families of Japanese descent, was forced to leave their home.

Courtesy City of Surrey Heritage Services (2001.0005.0001).

BERRY BASKET FROM OTA FAMILY FARM

Tell Me More

The family was forced to go to the Minto Internment Camp, located in an abandoned mining community near Lillooet. The interned families took over the empty houses and survived on their pre-war savings, finding jobs in trucking, logging, and the sawmill industry. Soon Minto's gravel flats became gardens. The produce was sold in nearby towns. While the families of Japanese descent were **imprisoned**, the Canadian government, under the War Measures Act, sold off their homes and belongings very cheaply and without their permission. After several hard years, the Ota family moved to the Surrey–Delta border area of Cedar Hills and began farming raspberries and strawberries again. They sold their crops at fresh produce markets and to canneries. Ray Ota stayed in the family berry farming business.

WOULD YOU BELIEVE?

Today, Surrey is home to almost 500 farms. They are an important part of the community, contributing to local farmers' markets and the city's economy. The city supports these farmers by protecting and expanding farmland.

My Turn

Would you like to try growing a pumpkin? It's a great plant to start gardening with.

1. Get some pumpkin seeds, a paper cup, and **compost.**

2. Fill the paper cup with compost.

3. Dig a hole in the compost 1.5 centimetres deep. Place three seeds in it. Cover the hole.

4. Water the seeds daily.

5. It will grow fast! Once it gets too big for the cup, you can replant it in your garden or a larger pot.

CONNECTIONS

Acadia was a thriving colony owned by the French in what we now call Nova Scotia. It began in 1605 in a town called Port Royal. Both the French and the English thought the colony was theirs and fought over it for years. Finally, in 1713, France signed it over to Britain. However, this didn't stop them fighting over the rest of North America. In 1754, during the French and Indian War, the British became scared the Acadians would work with France against them because of their shared roots. They forced the Acadians to leave the colony. Many died during the deportation. Some of the Acadians ended up in Spanish Louisiana and became known as the Cajuns. Today, Cajuns still speak a form of the old French they spoke in Acadia. They are famous for their cooking and their music called zydeco. You say it like this: zy-dih-koh!

WHY IS THE BERRY BASKET IMPORTANT IN THIS AREA?

Surrey has a long history of berry farming. Many early farmers in the area chose to grow berries between the large stumps left on the land following the **clear-cutting** of forests. By "stump farming," they could begin farming for less money. Many of these farmers were Japanese Canadian settlers. They formed a community in the areas now known as the Cedar and Strawberry Hills neighbourhoods. Sadly, after their wartime internment, few farmers were able to return to their Surrey farms.

JUST THE FACTS

WHAT IS IT? This wheel is from the *K de K* ferry, the first steam ferry that moved people (and their pets) between Surrey and New Westminster from 1883 to 1889.

WHAT DOES IT LOOK LIKE? It looks like a wooden hula hoop combined with a giant wooden star stuck to it.

WHERE DOES IT COME FROM? The *K de K* was built by Captain Angus Grant who named the ferry after his friend, Joseph Sexton Knyvett de Knyvett. How the piece got to the museum is unknown.

WHAT'S ITS STORY? Captain Grant's ferry licence was rented from the cities of Surrey and New Westminster. The ferry operated on an hourly basis from 6 a.m. to 8 p.m., from Monday through Saturday, with shorter hours on Sundays. It was a big asset for the people of Surrey. In the 1880s, New Westminster was the largest **economic** centre in the Lower Mainland. In comparison, Surrey was mostly a farming area. A steady way to cross the river meant more opportunity for the Surrey farmers, who were able to buy and sell in the bigger city.

Lower Mainland

> MUSEUM OF SURREY

K DE K FERRY WHEEL

Courtesy Surrey Archives (209.03).

Courtesy City of Surrey Heritage Services (1962.0254.0001).

Tell Me More

The location of the *K de K* ferry wharf, Surrey's only ferry wharf at the time, was purposely located in the riverside area of Brownsville, which is now known as Bridgeview. Brownsville was an important stopping point for rail, road, and trail travellers from Fort Langley, Surrey's lowlands, eastern Canada, and the United States. All these connecting transportation links made Brownsville Surrey's most important community and a busy place. It was filled with hotels, **livery stables**, and other well-paid businesses. It was even the first community in Surrey to have a telephone installed! Ferry fares were 35 cents return for anyone over 10 years old.

? WOULD YOU BELIEVE?

The ferry wasn't just for people. Small farm animals younger than 1 year old were ten cents each, while large farm animals were charged 25 cents each.

My Turn

The story of the ferry teaches us about how transportation can promote connection. Take a moment to think about all the types of public transportation you use, and how these connect you to the activities you love. Maybe you take a bus to hockey, or the SkyTrain to visit your cousins in the city, or a ferry to see your Aunt Agnes. How would you get to these places without these things? Just think about it.

CONNECTIONS

Did you know the longest free ferry ride in the world is in BC? It's the Kootenay Lake ferry and it runs between Balfour and Kootenay Bay. The crossing is eight kilometres long and takes 35 minutes. Service is all year long and boasts some gorgeous views. Thousands of people travel on the ferry each year on their way to go camping and exploring.

⭐ WHY IS THE FERRY WHEEL IMPORTANT IN THIS AREA?

The ferry played a huge role in linking Surrey with its larger neighbouring communities, as well as areas much further away. It's a big part of the community's history and added to the making of the area. Plus, it's a good example of how places change – just like people do – as they age. These days, not much is left of the original area of Brownsville, only some crumbling pilings and docks a little way from the SkyTrain bridge over the Fraser.

FRASER RIVER DISCOVERY CENTRE

JUST THE FACTS

WHERE IS IT? 788 Quayside Drive, New Westminster, V3M 6Z6
(604) 521-8401
https://fraserriverdiscovery.org
Fraser River Discovery Centre (FRDC) is located on the traditional territory of the Coast Salish Peoples.

ARE PHOTOGRAPHS ALLOWED? Yes, FRDC hosts monthly photography competitions where visitors can share their best photos of the Fraser, or the Discovery Centre!

HOW DID IT START? FRDC first took shape in 1989 when a group of people from business and environmental backgrounds created the Fraser River Discovery Centre Society. Fundraising to support the creation of the centre was done in coordination with the City of New Westminster. In 2001, a 465-metre Preview Centre opened for visitors along the New Westminster Quay. That's about one-third the size of a hockey rink. In 2009, FRDC reopened to visitors with about 1580 square metres of exhibit space. That's the size of three basketball courts.

WHERE HAS IT LIVED?
788 Quayside Drive has always been FRDC's home.

WHERE DO THE ITEMS COME FROM?
FRDC is more like an interpretive centre and activity space than a traditional museum. With a few exceptions, it relies on replicas, the views of the river itself, and custom-built exhibits to tell its stories. It does have some donated objects. One display contains swimming gear from Finn Donnelly, who swam the river twice, in 1995 and again in 2000, to raise awareness about water pollution. You can read his story a bit later in the book.

HOW HAS IT CHANGED?
The biggest change to FRDC was the opening of *Journey through the Working River* in 2017. This exhibit shows how the Fraser River supports 42,000 jobs in BC, but it also asks visitors to think about the positive and negative ways **economic activity** affects the river. In 2020, FRDC entered into a **memorandum of understanding** with the xʷməθkʷəy̓əm (Musqueam) First Nation. The first goal is to develop xʷtatəl̓ləm (pronounced hwa-ta-te-lum), a place of learning about the Indigenous heritage and teachings of the Fraser River. FRDC is committed to collaborating with First Nations of the Fraser River to share Indigenous ways of knowing from their own perspective about the river and its incredible biodiversity.

Image courtesy Fraser River Discovery Centre.

learn the importance of different types of watercraft on a river.

TUGGY THE TUGBOAT

Image courtesy Fraser River Discovery Centre.

Tuggy is a scaled-down model of the kind of tugboat that hauls **log booms** and guides large ships into port.

This tug was built specially for the exhibit *Journey through the Working River*, which opened in 2017.

Tugs are one of the most common sights on the Fraser River.

These boats are small but mighty. They can tow barges filled with logs, pulp and paper, lumber, and wood chips, or other bulky cargo like cement, railcars, and freight.

Tugs can pull barges that hold the equivalent of 65 truckloads of material. That means each barge keeps 65 trucks off the roads.

If an oil spill happens, tugboat pilots quickly move OSCAR (oil spill containment and recovery) trailers to the stretch of contaminated water. These trailers contain tools and materials needed to help stop the spread of harmful spills.

Without tugs, large ships have a hard time maneuvering in the river. Did you know some big ships take over one kilometre, or 15 minutes, to come to a complete stop?

Tugs have the pulling strength of 12 school buses. Their propellers can spin in any direction, which allows them to turn very quickly. Recycled airplane tires hanging over the sides of tugs protect them from river debris or from other boats that may accidently crash into them.

FIN DONNELLY'S FRASER RIVER SWIM GEAR

JUST THE FACTS

WHAT IS IT? This is the gear Fin Donnelly wore to swim the length of the Fraser River.

WHAT DOES IT LOOK LIKE? Fin wore an insulated wetsuit and swim cap, a life jacket, fins, and gloves.

WHERE DOES IT COME FROM? Fin donated his swim gear to FRDC for the exhibit *The Ripple Effect*, which told the story of his two marathon swims.

WHAT'S ITS STORY? In September 1995, Fin Donnelly wore this equipment when he swam the 1375-kilometre length of the Fraser River.

Tell Me More

Fin's gear was designed to keep him warm and afloat in the dangerous and freezing river, but he was constantly on the edge of hypothermia. When someone suffers from hypothermia, they get so cold their body can't warm itself up. Not only did he have to deal with the cold but he also had to adapt to water levels that kept changing. The tides of the Salish Sea constantly push and pull on the river water. Now imagine being cold, being pushed and pulled by currents, and swimming 20 days for 5 to 13 hours a day with only one rest day! That's what Fin did.

Image courtesy Fraser River Discovery Centre.

126

WOULD YOU BELIEVE?

In 1995, as Fin swam beneath the Pattullo Bridge by New Westminster near the estuary of the river, the pollution became so bad it stung his eyes through his goggles.

My Turn

What could you do to make people aware of an environmental problem in your community?

Fin Donnelly's story shows us how one person can make a big difference. News coverage of his swims and scientific articles about the Fraser River pressured companies to become more environmentally friendly. After his 1995 swim, he helped create the **not-for-profit** Rivershed Society of BC, which encourages the public to learn about the Fraser River Basin. The Fraser River passes through ten biogeoclimactic zones. Within each zone there is similar plant and animal life, rock formations, and climate. There are 12 biogeoclimactic zones in BC, so it's pretty amazing the Fraser River passes through ten of them! The society also offers scholarships to young people for an outdoor education program that takes them on rafts, canoes, and on foot from the Fraser River headwaters to the estuary. They learn how to connect to, protect, and restore watersheds like the Fraser. Now a Member of the Legislative Assembly (MLA) in BC, Fin Donnelly is still working to protect BC's waters.

★ WHY IS FIN DONNELLY'S SWIM GEAR IMPORTANT IN THIS AREA?

After Fin finished university, he wondered how he could make a difference, especially when it came to the environment. He thought he could make people aware of the health of the Fraser River by swimming from Port Coquitlam to the Pacific Ocean, about 372 kilometres. However, as he told others about his plan, they told him of problems further and further up the river. He finally decided to start his swim at Tête Jaune Cache, an important spawning area for chinook salmon. He held fundraisers and community events to draw attention to disappearing salmon runs, loss of wetlands, and increasing silt and chemicals in the river. Although the Fraser is still fairly wild, economic and industrial growth has increased pollution. You would think making a swim like this once was enough, but Donnelly swam the length of the Fraser River again in 2000.

JUST THE FACTS

WHAT IS IT? This is a Coast Salish dip net for catching Pacific salmon.

WHAT DOES IT LOOK LIKE? It has a long cedar pole with a hoop at the end. The hoop holds a net made of hemp rope. The net is attached to the pole using rings made from deer backbone. A long string trails down from the hoop.

WHERE DOES IT COME FROM? This net has never been used, but it is made from the same materials used by Indigenous fishers in the Fraser River Canyon. It was donated to FRDC in 2012 for the *Our Bones Are Made of Salmon* exhibit.

WHAT'S ITS STORY? The Stó:lō First Nation has lived and fished both in the Fraser Canyon and the Fraser Valley since time immemorial and continues to do so using traditional fishing methods.

Tell Me More

The fisher stands over the river, holding the dip net in a spot of calm water between rushing rapids. Salmon heading upriver like to stop in these calmer spots to rest during their journey. As they wait for salmon, the fisher holds on to the string that keeps the net open. After a salmon swims into the net, the fisher lets go of the string, which causes the net to get pulled with the current and snap shut, trapping the fish. This fishing technique requires constant energy and strength because the fisher must lift the salmon from a long distance below them.

Image courtesy Fraser River Discovery Centre.

COAST SALISH DIP NET

Information on Indigenous fishing tools and practices has been generously shared with FRDC by Musqueam Elder Larry Grant and Stó:lō Cultural Advisor Dr. Sonny McHalsie.

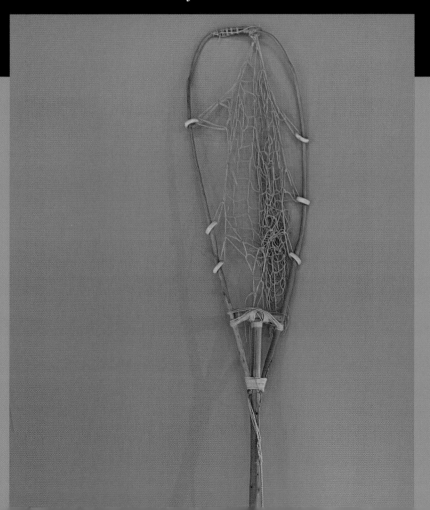

WOULD YOU BELIEVE?

After catching salmon, fishers preserve the fish using their natural surroundings in the Fraser Canyon. They hang their salmon up to dry in huge rows and the wind does the rest of the work.

My Turn

The Stó:lō First Nation says their bones are made from salmon. What do you eat that makes your bones strong?

CONNECTIONS

The river is so closely tied to Stó:lō culture that their name, Stó:lō, means "river" in the Coast Salish language Halq'eméylem (Halkomelem). Seeing how these traditional fishing methods are still used helps us understand that Indigenous cultures are still here and continue to be an important part of west coast history. Yes, this fishing technique is thousands of years old, but it is still used successfully today.

WHY IS THE DIP NET IMPORTANT IN THIS AREA?

Oral histories and origin stories of Indigenous communities along the river say they have been here since time immemorial. They have no stories of arriving to this region from somewhere else, and so have always been here. From archeological evidence, we know that about 85 per cent of the protein in the diets of Coast Salish Peoples came from marine sources. Their bones are literally made from salmon. Salmon fishing was, and still is, an important economic and cultural practice for Indigenous Peoples. In many communities, when the first salmon of the season is caught, an important ceremony takes place thanking the river for providing the people with everything they require.

JUST THE FACTS

FISH DRYING RACK

WHAT IS IT? This is a traditional Indigenous rack for wind-drying fish.

WHAT DOES IT LOOK LIKE? A tripod at each end of the rack supports two rails from which fish are hung to dry.

WHERE DOES IT COME FROM? The rack is part of the exhibit *Our Bones Are Made of Salmon*. It was built with the assistance of two Indigenous Elders: Larry Grant from Musqueam First Nation near the mouth of the Fraser River, and Sonny McHalsie from Stó:lō First Nation in the Fraser Valley. They shared their Traditional Knowledge of salmon fishing and what the river means to them.

WHAT'S ITS STORY? Both of these First Nations still use this type of drying rack.

Image courtesy Fraser River Discovery Centre.

Tell Me More

As soon as a salmon is caught, its head is removed and its body turned upside down to bleed for about ten minutes. The salmon are carried to the drying rack where they are gutted and prepared for drying. The technique for preparing the salmon is passed down through mothers and grandmothers, and each family has a different method. These days the tail is usually taken off, then the salmon is hung on the rack using a string to allow the fillets to spin for better air circulation and quicker drying time.

? WOULD YOU BELIEVE?

The Fraser River Canyon is one of the only places along the river where salmon can be prepared using the wind-drying method. The sun heats up the canyon walls and they become very hot. This creates gusts of warm air that are funnelled down the canyon, perfect for drying fish so it can be eaten or stored for later.

My Turn

What reasons can you think of for using this traditional fishing technology?

CONNECTIONS

Indigenous Peoples say they have lived along the river since time immemorial. Their method of drying fish is thousands of years old, yet it is still used today. Why do you think this is?

★ WHY IS THE FISH DRYING RACK IMPORTANT IN THIS AREA?

Depending on the weather and the location of the drying rack, fish will take between six and 14 days to dry. By hanging salmon on racks in the hot, dry Fraser Canyon air, Indigenous Peoples can prepare thousands of fillets at a time, which in the past saw them through the winter months and provided something to trade with other communities. Wind-dried salmon can last up to a year, much longer than smoked salmon.

JUST THE FACTS

WHAT IS IT? This is a replica or model of a fish called a white sturgeon.

WHAT DOES IT LOOK LIKE? George is dark on top, and he has a silver belly and sides. Along his spine and just below his dark grey back, he has diamond-shaped markings that run from his head to his tail. These sharp bony plates that are like armour are called scutes.

WHERE DOES IT COME FROM? This replica was made for FRDC by the Fraser River Sturgeon Conservation Society.

WHAT'S ITS STORY? White sturgeon were once popular with both recreational and commercial fishers. Overfishing almost wiped out the white sturgeon population on the Fraser River. This fish was about 40 years old when it was caught.

Image courtesy Fraser River Discovery Centre.

Lower Mainland

> **FRASER RIVER DISCOVERY CENTRE**

GEORGE THE WHITE STURGEON

Tell Me More

Would you believe that white sturgeon have been around since the time of the dinosaurs? It is the largest freshwater fish in Canada and looks almost exactly like it did millions of years ago. Unlike the dinosaurs, white sturgeon survived volcanoes and ice ages. In the lower Fraser River, some white sturgeon grow to be six metres in length. That's about three times the length of a king-size bed. They can weigh up to 800 kilograms, as much as a full-grown male grizzly bear and more than a full-grown moose. A white sturgeon reaching that length and weight may be more than 100 years old!

WOULD YOU BELIEVE?

The sturgeon's mouth looks a bit like a flexible vacuum hose. Large white sturgeon can extend their mouths up to half a metre wide.

My Turn

White sturgeon are not the only animals to survive from the time of the dinosaurs. Can you find five other living creatures that were around with the dinosaurs?

CONNECTIONS

Wouldn't it be awful if a fish that has survived millions of years were to disappear from our planet? Since 2000, the Fraser River Sturgeon Conservation Society has trained volunteers to tag, sample, and release live sturgeon in the lower Fraser. Using these recording methods, scientists can keep track of the number of white sturgeon in the Fraser River.

WHY IS THE WHITE STURGEON IMPORTANT IN THIS AREA?

White sturgeon are an important part of the Fraser River food chain. They are a key predator and feed on anything and everything. Juveniles root in rocks and sand for snails and other **invertebrates**. As they grow, sturgeon begin feeding on larger fish such as salmon and eulachon. According to government of Canada reports, the numbers of juvenile white sturgeon are falling. Loss of habitat (a place to live) is one reason, but so is the effect of industry and agriculture on water quality. Combined with the effects of climate change and the numbers of salmon and eulachon, some of the sturgeon's food sources have also been reduced.

WHAT COULD I DO IN A MUSEUM?

Josh Doherty   Winter Stacey

INTERVIEW WITH JOSH DOHERTY, FABRICATION DESIGN MANAGER, AND WINTER STACEY, FABRICATION COORDINATOR, MUSEUM OF VANCOUVER

INTERVIEWER: Tell me, what do you do?

JOSH: My job is to take an empty gallery and put an exhibit in it. Finding out where the artifacts go and finding ways to display them, while keeping them safe from sun and people. The curatorial department has the story it wants to tell, and we get to tell it visually.

WINTER: My background is theatre. I did that through high school, building and painting sets. At the museum, we are creating a set for people to walk through. But it's more of an immersive set and it's longer lasting, so it has more of an impact. You have to think about what impact you have to make with your long-term set. We make the room fit the objects.

INTERVIEWER: Talk a little about safety.

JOSH: So, as a museum, our job is to preserve pieces of history, and we have a responsibility to make sure our objects decay as slowly as possible.

WINTER: We have two responsibilities. We want to display and show the objects that have been given to us. And then we must keep them as safe as possible so they can be displayed forever in beauty. Because everything has a life, right?

INTERVIEWER: What's the hardest part of your job?

JOSH: Working with other people is both the hardest part and one of the best parts.

WINTER: And working with different cultures too. It's learning what is ok to display and how to display it to be as totally respectful as possible.

JOSH: A couple of exhibits back, we were including paddles. The Tsleil-Waututh Nation was very assertive that their paddles could not be displayed with the blades down. That was something we had to learn.

INTERVIEWER: What's the best part of your job?

WINTER: You're never doing the same thing for longer than a week. It's always different. Some people don't like that. But it's the perfect thing for me. You never get bored of one thing for long.

JOSH: I like to get really immersed into something for a period of time and then get right out of it.

INTERVIEWER: How much of what a visitor sees in the gallery is up to you?

WINTER: It really depends on the exhibition. Some curators have a really strong idea about what they want the exhibition to look and feel like. Others haven't got a clear idea and want more input from us.

JOSH: The exhibit *All We Want Is More: The Tobias Wong Project* was kind of my idea. I got to run with that one.

WINTER: The placement of the objects was also more of a conversation leading up to the exhibit. The curator showed us the objects and their cultural significance. We were like, "Ok, so what shouldn't go into cases together? Here is a 'nice' object, and here is a 'bad' object. Maybe we should put the 'bad' things all together so you can experience it all at once."

JOSH: Yeah. And that's fun too, to be a part of that conversation. It's not just black and white. It's like, "What do you guys think?"

INTERVIEWER: If a kid wanted to do what you do, what could they be doing now to prepare?

WINTER: Designing anything they can come up with. Learn how to sketch. It's the most important part. How can you get what's in your head across to other people? If you want to make a backpack, draw the backpack. Just try it.

JOSH: And then make it in cardboard. You'll learn pretty quickly what doesn't work. We like cardboard and green painter's tape and hot glue.

WINTER: The goal is to get to the actual size of things as quickly as possible. If we're trying to think about a room where we're going to build some walls, we tape out walls on the floor. Then we can see, "Oh, this is too big, or, oh, this is too small, or, yeah, this will work."

INTERVIEWER: Winter, you came in through theatre. Tell me about that.

WINTER: I wanted to be involved in theatre when I was in elementary school, but acting was scary. I remember forgetting my lines in one play, and that was kind of it for me. I was like, that was way too much. So, in high school, I was lucky enough to go to a school that was very theatre-focused and it was Grades 8 to 12. Everyone was involved from ticket sales, ushers, to the pre-show, which was always the film class showing their movies. We got to be involved in the costumes, in makeup, and I moseyed my way into the stage sets, which was the best place to be, the most fun. We'd say, "Does this look right now? I think we need some more of this. Oh, that looks better." And I was like…freedom.

INTERVIEWER: And you, Josh?

JOSH: I've always made things. My grandpa had me in his workshop when I was a little kid. I directed him 'cause I couldn't use the table saw. But I did work in machine shops and then went to Emily Carr and did the industrial design program. And accidentally got into museums because one of my classmate's dads was sort of a roving conservator and mount maker. So I started making mounts.

WINTER: Which are things that hold an object. The most heartbreaking thing is you put so much effort and time into a mount just for it to not be seen.

JOSH: So lots of metal work, woodwork, and making things, putzing around with electronics and then industrial design at Emily Carr.

INTERVIEWER: That's a really good thing for kids to hear. You know, what you just said about putzing around with things like building things and making things.

WINTER: You said you used to take apart radios to see how they would work.

JOSH: Yeah, stuff like that. Just being interested.

WINTER: You can always break stuff and try to fix it again. And I guess that's another thing. Be a weirdo. Like, "What's this thing in this pile of trash?" And just want to know more and want to know how things work. If kids can do that, I think they can do a lot of things they never thought they could do. Nobody ever wants to be told to volunteer in order to work. But if you're interested in these things, get involved when you're young because that can be that foot in the door when you graduate. Make your passion the job.

Joëlle Sévigny

INTERVIEW WITH JOËLLE SÉVIGNY, FORMER PROGRAM AND EDUCATION MANAGER, QATHET MUSEUM & ARCHIVES

Joëlle's work centred on public outreach, education, and programming. She often writes articles about the history of the qathet Regional District for publications such as *qathet Living* magazine.

INTERVIEWER: Tell me about your work at the museum?

JOËLLE: I developed and delivered educational programs at the museum for people of all ages. Some of these programs took the form of workshops, speaker series, memoir writing programs, summer camps for youth, and more! Part of my job was also to partner with other like-minded community organizations and to promote the museum and its activities. Overall, my goal was to educate and engage both residents and visitors in the history of the qathet Regional District, which the qathet Museum & Archives represents.

INTERVIEWER: What did you like best about your job?

JOËLLE: What I liked best about my job was the opportunity to be creative! I love finding ways to teach the public about history in a manner that is informal and fun. Hands-on activities are always great for this, for example, learning about paper by making our own, or learning about archeology by simulating an excavation. Creating these programs was my favourite part of my work.

INTERVIEWER: Is there anything that might surprise people about your job?

JOËLLE: Even though my primary job at the museum was programming, in smaller community museums you end up doing a little bit of everything. I also worked with the collections, donations, and exhibits, writing grants and tracking expenses, and responding to researchers and completing research inquiries. I worked in many departments and areas of the museum.

INTERVIEWER: Is there anything you didn't like about your job?

JOËLLE: A lot goes on behind the scenes to plan and develop programs. There is a lot of research, preparation, as well as administrative tasks that go along with it. This means sometimes I had to work at a computer desk for long periods of time. This **sedentary** aspect of my job was my least favourite.

INTERVIEWER: Do you like writing about history? Is it hard?

JOËLLE: I find it very fulfilling to write about the past in the hope that readers learn something new or perhaps spark their own memory. I was always an avid reader growing up, and so writing comes naturally to me. It is a skill I further developed at school and also in my free time writing adventure stories. I find the most difficult and time-consuming part is the research. Writing history is sort of like detective work: reading various reference books, looking through archival documents, and finding as many clues as possible.

INTERVIEWER: Did you always want to want to work in a museum?

JOËLLE: I first had a very romanticized view of working in the field of history, largely due to watching popularized television shows and movies. In my youth, I envisioned myself becoming the female counterpart of Indiana Jones, with a mix of Dr. Brennan [from the TV show *Bones*], a physical and forensic anthropologist. And so, with this dream in mind, I first became an archeologist, with a concentration in physical anthropology. I soon realized it wasn't quite like the movies pictured it. I very much enjoyed the field but found few employment opportunities in this line of work. I then turned to museum studies. I started working as a student at a historical site in a living house museum. In the summer I gave tours of the historic district to visitors and found I quite enjoyed sharing my passion for history with others. Soon afterwards, I was hired as an educator in a small community museum where I was able to further engage with the public.

INTERVIEWER: When you were a kid, did you like history?

JOËLLE: My favourite subject growing up was science. I had a laboratory kit and loved examining things under my microscope. I enjoyed biology since my family spent a lot of time outside, my parents always taking the time to explain to us the fauna and flora. My interest in history started when I began to read historical adventure novels. The intrigue of exploring a fantasy world grounded in some amount of true facts was very exciting! Part of the excitement was also learning about how different people lived in different time periods. This eventually translated to liking history, but I was particularly interested in how humans evolved through time, how they lived in the past, and I wanted to gain a better understanding of the different cultures in the world.

INTERVIEWER: What advice would you give kids interested in working at a museum?

JOËLLE: Many museums have volunteer programs, which is a great opportunity to gain hands-on experience and see what working in a museum environment is like. There are also many different streams in the museum field, so if you can, try a little bit of everything to find out what you like best! If volunteering is not an option, I suggest becoming a member of your local museum, participating in programs offered and finding opportunities to speak to museum workers about their careers. When you travel or go out of town, you can also visit other museums to see various types of museum settings.

Alison Pascal

INTERVIEW WITH ALISON PASCAL, CURATOR, SQUAMISH LÍL'WAT CULTURAL CENTRE

INTERVIEWER: We're here to talk about the Indigenous Youth Ambassador Program.

ALISON: The Indigenous Youth Ambassador Program was created even before we had a cultural centre. The Chiefs and Councils from both Nations, when they decided to build a cultural centre, knew our own Indigenous People had very little experience talking about our culture with non-Indigenous people, and it would be best to have some experience before the cultural centre opened. We've done performances, but not the interpretation side of things and not the programming side of things. So already the leadership knew we needed to work on that and they decided to create programs and education opportunities working in tourism.

INTERVIEWER: How did they do that?

ALISON: The Squamish Nation had been working on this program, an environmental stewardship program. It was really geared to getting the youth onto the land. That program is considered to be the first Indigenous Youth Ambassador Program because everything we have at the cultural centre all started from that. The Squamish Nation thought getting the youth into the program was a really good start, but they really needed to make it feasible to run long-term. This one idea didn't have a revenue generator, or a long-lasting career for the youth. And so they started to look at different options.

INTERVIEWER: What options did they explore?

ALISON: They had worked with not just getting the youth onto the land but having the youth the next year work at some of the different parks within the Squamish Nation. That was the first year that Indigenous People got to take ownership back over some of the Crown land parks. The youth worked at some of the different parks, managing the campsites, cleaning, taking bookings, taking the payment, and repairing some of the infrastructure. In Squamish, they had Alice Lake, Cat Lake, and Brohm Lake. Some of them were known as party lakes. So a lot of the youth from Vancouver or the suburbs would come up after graduation and enjoy their new-found freedom. It wasn't a really great fit. The interaction between the Nation members and the customers wasn't always respectful.

INTERVIEWER: What was the solution?

ALISON: They decided the year after to work at some of the different tourist destinations. They settled on Shannon Falls, and this time they had a salmon cart there, so they had a little food cart where they sold salmon wraps, salmon Caesar salad, I think. It was a better fit. Oh yeah, they ran the food cart in conjunction with an art project.

INTERVIEWER: An art project? What kind?

ALISON: They had one of their master carvers come down and they were working on a ten-foot carving. They were able to have the youth working with their hands, learning about one of the traditional crafts of the Nation. But they were also working on speaking with visitors and interpreting the culture. In the Sea-to-Sky Corridor, you know, logging was the main industry for a long time, but by the 2000s, we had really switched to tourism. And so everybody thought, ok, we're a tourism-based, visitor-experience corridor. They found that the youth developed the ability to interact while creating this environment, where they could celebrate their culture and celebrate their history and kind of start to move away from all of the shame-based experiences they might have had in public school.

INTERVIEWER: So where did the cultural centre come in?

ALISON: By that time, they knew about the cultural centre, so they had a goal in mind. They started to focus on customer experience, creating programs we could possibly run here. But it was really about being able to talk about our culture and share that with visitors. Once we got the cultural centre up and running, then you know the certificate side of things was always there. They just really enhanced and really chose some great programs like FOODSAFE, first aid, and the Workers' Compensation Board work safe program. People come in, talk about financials and financial health and getting people set up with budgets because, you know, that's not really covered in public school.

INTERVIEWER: That's so true.

ALISON: We have worked with WorkBC. The people that help you find jobs. So they come in, and they help with resume building, cover letters, job searches, or they talk about what that individual wants to do and help set them on a path to finding that. And the whole goal is for the participants to further their career by having another job or going back into school by the end of the program.

INTERVIEWER: This is a 12-week program, is that right?

ALISON: The weeks change depending on funding. It's been as short as eight, as long as 16, but it's a good chunk of time that we have youth with us. On the other side of things, what really makes this program special and unique is it is open to all Indigenous People, not just the Squamish or Líl'wat Nations, but we do focus on Squamish and Líl'wat Nation culture. So, while they're here, they get all of those really great job certificates that they can go out and use that translate easily to any kind of business you want to work in. They also get to do job shadowing in the gift shop, in the café, and in the catering department. If they are really interested, you know there's always maintenance. And a little bit of marketing, like, we don't really get too far into sales and marketing. They do get to meet our workers and talk about what they do and how they got started in those positions, but those are not entry-level jobs, so they just get to do some social media posts or things like that. Write some blogs. But they do spend a lot of time with customer experience. They work with our ambassadors and work the front desk and get cash handling. They also work on delivering tours. In the Cultural Growth and Sharing team, our goal is to be able to have our trainees start to deliver tours by the end of the program so that they're really confident in public speaking and they really learn a lot of the culture and stories and have that ability to share songs.

INTERVIEWER: That's really amazing.

ALISON: Yeah, it's really a great program. It kind of creates a tight bond between the participants because they're doing so much learning. All of the students have different backgrounds. Not everybody is fortunate to grow up with a family that participates in the culture. So we've had some of our Nation members that live in the city, in Vancouver, and they're not able to join in the culture as much in their younger days. It's really nice for them to be able to come here and learn all of those things, and it's really nice they are able to learn it without judgment.

INTERVIEWER: Could you explain that a little bit?

ALISON: One of the biggest things we hear is that a lot of [Indigenous] People are afraid to go into the community and talk about how little they know of the language or how little they know of the culture. It's one of the really hard things about the legacies of residential school – that feeling of inadequacy. It still exists today, but you know, we always tell them, "We all started somewhere."

Most of the staff at the cultural centre have gone through the youth program. And so we're saying, "You know, I joined the program too. I learned a lot. Nobody knows everything, and everybody's family has their own specialties, so you've got something to share with us and we have something to share with you."

INTERVIEWER: What is the average age for participants?

ALISON: Technically, you can sign up at 16, but really the program is geared for people who have left high school because our programs run starting in September and ending in December, and then we just started a program mid-February and that will end before the summer. It's really for those that have left high school, young adults, kind of like venturing into finding their path in life.

INTERVIEWER: What will they do after the program?

ALISON: It's really split, and it's really tough to get further education. A lot of people are hesitant to leave the reserve, I think, if they haven't had any experience living away from the family. A lot of people have trouble with the rental market and inflation. Leaving the reserve is sometimes unfeasible. You have to have a roommate to live somewhere safe and a job and this long-term plan. A lot of times people will find jobs through some of our affiliates. We introduce the youth to different businesses and let them know what's going on. It's really great that way. In the Líl'wat Nation we do have the Tszil Learning Centre, which is right in our community, where you can take some of those university courses or college courses to get you up to speed and get you used to the program. Eventually, you have to go to the city to finish programs. We find it just gives people that confidence in their ability to create for themselves a safety net or a family outside of the family. It's actually one of our taglines: "Apply for a job and find a family."

INTERVIEWER: I read on your website that the youth work with Elders and Knowledge Keepers. So what types of things might they do?

ALISON: When we have Elders coming in, they're talking about cultural protocols or a lot to do with drumming and singing. We do have a lot of Knowledge Keepers that are not in the Elder category but have specialized family knowledge that we ask them to share. So they do drum making, cedar weaving, carving, Salish wool weaving. I think this year they're doing clay pottery. They've done fish skin tanning and a whole variety of things, depending on who is available and what time of year it is.

ALISON: It's really a wide variety. We do have a lot that go into trades – construction, the food industry. A few in administration. A couple have gone into leadership, like Chief and Council. We have one who is a graduate of Capilano University in communications or political science. One of her long-term goals is to be a councilman or a mayor. But one of her shorter-term goals was to be in the US Navy because her father was in the navy. Currently, she is in the navy. She lives in Virginia. She's studying dental hygiene while serving her term. Because we do a lot of cultural training, they do end up working for the public school system as Indigenous support workers. A couple have actually gone to become certified teachers, so that's really great to see.

ALISON: The one thing I would add is the program is managed by former participants, both the manager of the program and the supervisor. They graduated from the Indigenous Youth Ambassador Program.

ALISON: We do. We hire through Canada Summer Jobs. So, yeah, we have one in the curatorial department, usually one in marketing and maintenance, and also one for the Cultural Delivery or Cultural Growth and Sharing team.

TWENTY WAYS YOU CAN USE THIS BOOK

1. With others, pick an image from one of the two-page spreads and play the game I spy.

2. Make up an alphabet game using items from the museums. For example, find all the items starting with the letter "a," then "b," and so on. Are there any letters missing?

3. Choose a museum and play a guessing game. For example, using the Fraser River Discovery Centre: "I am long, have gills, and live a long time. What am I?" (A sturgeon.)

4. Use the glossary to learn new words. Pick a word of the day.

5. Use the boldfaced words in the book to create a word game. Each person in a group looks up the definition of their word and then makes up two more definitions. The others have to guess the correct one.

6. Find the location of a museum or centre on a map. Then find out everything you can about the nearest town or city.

7. Pick your favourite item in the book. Think about all the possible ways it could be used. For example, the egg carton was designed to hold eggs, but you could also use it to plant seedlings or organize different-sized screws.

8. Go to the library or use the computer to do additional research about an item.

9. Many items are described with measurements. To get a better idea of how large or small an item is, compare it to a school bus. The average school bus is 10.66 metres long and 2.5 metres wide. For weight, compare the weight of the item to your own weight, or the weight of your parents/guardians or friends.

10. Practise categorizing. How many different categories does one item fit into? How few categories could be used to describe all the items in the book?

11. Take on the role of a reporter and create a list of questions you would ask the museum/centre curator about some of the items you've read about.

12. What's your favourite? Pick your favourite item, picture, word, or fact in the book. Why is it your favourite?

13. Many museums in the world still "own" objects taken from cultures and peoples without their consent. Should museums return these objects? Why or why not?

14. Compare two items from different museums and centres and see if you can find any similarities between them.

15. Visit a museum that isn't in this book. Pick an item and take pictures of it (if you are allowed). Research and write about the item, then design a new page for this book.

16. Think of a new subtitle for information you think should be added to the item descriptions in the book.

17. Visit a museum included in the book and find other items you think should have been added.

18. Find out what colours occur most frequently in First Nations items. What colours, if any, are missing?

19. Look through the book and find the items that may still exist where you live (town, city, province).

20. Ask each member of your family or group of friends to pick an item they own and have them explain why it belongs in a museum. Each person could then make a new page for the book, describing their item.

AFTERWORD

Now that you've read our book, tell us, what items stood out for you? What things made you think differently? Were you surprised by what these objects taught you about the past? Maybe there was something you wish you owned? Did anything make you want to search for old treasures, or ask your grandma or grandad about the things they used as kids? What did these belongings teach you about the present or the future? What items filled your imagination with ideas, made you want to invent things? We know, we know, we ask a lot of questions. We're kind of nosy, that's probably why we're writers. We're curious.

You probably know the belongings in a museum aren't just thrown in there all higgledy-piggledy. It's not by chance things end up there. It's not magic. There are many people who work in the museum and help make decisions about what visitors like you are going to see. Items are included because of their stories. These stories might be as different as a salamander and tractor, but each has something important to say.

While writing this book, we learned a lot about what it's like to work in a museum. Making a book uses a lot of the same skills. We had to decide which items we wanted in the book and what we had to leave out. We simply didn't have enough room for every story. Imagine the size of that book. Can you picture carrying that book around? It would probably weigh as much as a family of mammoths. Of course, that would be too heavy! Still, these were difficult decisions. Each object we reviewed revealed something new to us. Our advice is, if you can, try and visit these museums and others. You'll be amazed by what you discover about our province and yourself.

ACKNOWLEDGEMENTS

The authors would like to thank the following people and organizations for their time and generosity in creating this book:

BULKLEY VALLEY MUSEUM

Kira Westby, Curator

KSAN HISTORICAL VILLAGE AND MUSEUM

Pat Marshall, Henry Thomas Davis, and Michael David Schwan, for their assistance with translations

KITIMAT MUSEUM & ARCHIVES

Louise Avery, Executive Director

HLI GOOTHL WILP-ADOKSHL NISGA'A (NISGA'A MUSEUM)

Theresa Schober, Director and Curator

Kaitlyn Stephens, Collections Management Assistant, with the support of the Nisga'a Museum team

SQUAMISH LÍL'WAT CULTURAL CENTRE

Mixalhítsa7, Alison Pascal, Curator

Tmícwts'a, Irene Terry Peters, for the wonderfully informative tour

SUNSHINE COAST MUSEUM & ARCHIVES

Jess Silvey, SCMA Board of Directors

Allie Bartlett, Curatorial Assistant

Matthew Lovegrove, Curator

QATHET MUSEUM & ARCHIVES

Present and former staff at qathet Museum & Archives Society

MUSEUM OF VANCOUVER

Viviane Gosselin, Director of Collections & Exhibitions, Curator of Contemporary Culture

Jillian Povarchook, Former Curatorial Associate

Bérangère Descamps

Christine Pennington, Curatorial Associate

Sharon Fortney, Curator of Indigenous Collections and Engagement

Tracy Williams, Sesemiya, Squamish Nation

Leateeqwhia Daniels, Squamish Nation Language & Cultural Affairs Department, Curriculum Development

Josh Doherty, Fabrication Design Manager

Winter Stacey, Fabrication Coordinator

MUSEUM OF ANTHROPOLOGY AT UBC

Dr. Susan Rowley, Director

Dr. Jennifer Kramer, Curator, Pacific Northwest

Dr. Fuyubi Nakamura, Curator, Asia

Dr. Nesrine Basheer, Assistant Professor of Teaching, Department of Asian Studies

Osama El Bietar, Administrator, Muslim Association of Canada Centre, Vancouver

Dr. Karen Duffek, Curator, Contemporary Visual Arts and Pacific Northwest

HISTORIC JOY KOGAWA HOUSE

Ann-Marie Metten, Founding Executive Director of the Historic Joy Kogawa House Society

Ksenia Makaganova

Todd Wong

Joan Shigeko Young

Joy Kogawa and the Kogawa family for their stewardship of this cultural heritage site

SCIENCE WORLD

Teresa Virani, Chief Experience & Marketing Officer

Kiki Kirkpatrick, Program Manager

Parker McLean, Curator and Youth Program Specialist

Dana Turner, Nature and Sustainability Programs Manager

Romila Barryman

MISSION MUSEUM

Jennifer Nundal, Museum Manager

Courtney Miller, Former Museum Manager

BRITANNIA SHIPYARDS NATIONAL HISTORIC SITE

The City of Richmond

MUSEUM OF SURREY

Lynn Saffery, Museum Manager

Kristin Hardie, Heritage Manager

Louisa Smith, Curator of Collections

Linda Montague, Textiles Specialist

Alexandra Feakes, Collections Assistant

FRASER RIVER DISCOVERY CENTRE

Michael Goodchild

Alex Johansen, Public Engagement Coordinator

MONOVA MUSEUM & ARCHIVES OF NORTH VANCOUVER

Christy Brain, Reference Historian

GLOSSARY

abalone: Sea snails found in cold water with very colourful shells that were used for decoration.

accessible: A place that is easy to get to for all people.

acquired: Bought or obtained. Belongings were often purchased from Indigenous People for less than they were worth at a time when they did not have much money (often due to government laws and restrictions). They needed to sell some of their treasures in order to house, feed, and clothe their families.

agriculturalist: Another word for farmer.

ancestors: Those in your family who came before you.

appliquéd: Using pieces of fabric to create a picture.

archeologist: Someone who studies our history by looking at found objects from the past.

archives: A place where historical records are kept.

artifacts: Objects of artistic, cultural, or historical interest.

astronomer: A person who studies the sun, moon, stars, and other natural objects in space.

baleen: Found in toothless whales, baleen is made up of slats of keratin (the same protein found in fingernails). These slats help the whale filter food from water.

bedrock: Base or core.

biodiversity: Variety in living things like plants, insects, animals, and birds.

calligraphy: A way of making artistic-looking writing.

camphor: A powder or oil that has a strong smell and bitter taste.

cast: A copy of an original using a mold and a plastic-like material.

Chilkat: A type of woven robe with long fringe.

clear-cutting: When a logging company cuts down all the trees in an area.

co-curated: When people work together to pick stories, films, performers, or objects for an exhibition, festival, or show.

collaborative: When two or more people work together to create something.

colonizers: People who came from other countries and settled in what we now call Canada. Canada was a British colony.

commissioned: Paying a person to create something for you, for example a work of art.

compost: A mix of decomposing plant, food waste, organic materials, and manure that plants love to grow in.

computer programming: The process of designing and making a working program for a computer.

computing hardware: Parts of a computer.

confiscated: Removed from the owner's possession for a limited time period.

contagious: Something easily spread.

contemporary: Modern.

cowpox: A skin disease linked to touching an infected animal, usually rodents or cats.

cultural protocols: The rules or expected behaviours of a culture.

cultures: Customs, laws, dress, architectural style, and traditions.

curators: People who develop and care for a collection in a museum.

Custodian of Enemy Property: A government official whose job was to control the selling of property belonging to people the government considered the enemy.

data entry: Entering information into a system.

deportation: When a person is forced to leave a country.

descendant: A person related to an ancestor.

descent: A person's family background.

devastating: Damaging.

diatomaceous earth: A chalk-like sedimentary rock created from a fossilized type of algae.

disabilities: Conditions that make it difficult for people to do certain tasks. These can affect thinking, development, the physical body and its senses, or a combination of a few factors.

dislodge: Knock out of position.

diverse: Different.

document: Write about.

economic: The making of, selling of, and use of goods and services.

economic activity: Activities like shipping, agriculture, forestry, and recreation.

economy: How a group of people in an area sells and buys goods and services.

enthusiasts: People interested in an activity or sport.

environmental stewardship: Taking care of the natural environment through sustainable practices and conservation.

equestrian: To do with horses or horse riding.

equilibrium: Balance.

evolution: Gradual development or change.

feminist: Someone who believes in complete equality for women.

fibre art: Art using natural or human-made materials.

fraying: Edges of fabric that unravel.

gun emplacement: A concrete support onto which a large gun was mounted during the Second World War.

head tax: A fee charged to Chinese people wanting to move to Canada.

hereditary lineages: Family ancestry; those who came before.

heritage: Our traditions and the meaning we find in them (noun). An old building with links to our past (adjective).

heyday: A time of success.

historian: A person who studies and describes the past by looking at old things.

holistic: All the parts of something and how they connect to each other.

hulls: The leafy green part of a strawberry.

imprisoned: Being kept in a place against your will.

inclusive: Not leaving anyone out.

Indigenous: The earliest known people to have lived in an area.

initiates: Those who are learning.

inoculant: Something introduced into the human body to make it safe from a disease.

internment camp: During the Second World War, starting in 1942, the government of Canada took houses and businesses away from Japanese Canadians living close to the west coast and sent them to camps in the interior of BC.

intricately: In a very complicated or detailed way.

invertebrates: Animals that don't have backbones.

legacy: Something that is left to future generations so they can learn about and better understand a person, place, or thing.

livery stables: Where people can rent horses or rent a stable for their horse.

log booms: Floating logs connected in chains that act like fences to catch logs that have been forested. Sometimes the ends of the chains are attached to a tugboat so the whole boom can be pulled to a new location.

mass deportation: When a group of people are forced to leave their homes.

mass produce: Made in large amounts, usually in a factory on an assembly line.

Matriarchs: A female head of the family.

mechanical: The parts of the machine.

memorabilia: Old objects kept because of their connection to the past.

memorandum of understanding: An agreement between two parties.

mentor: A teacher or trusted advisor.

minority: A small group of people who are different culturally, ethnically, or racially from the majority of the people in a place.

mobilities: Describes different ways people move through the world, including using wheelchairs or other aids.

molten: Made liquid by heat.

multicultural: A society with people from many different cultures.

municipal: Relating to a town or district or its government.

narratives: Spoken or written stories.

national significance: An area, building, place, or person that tells a country's important stories.

Nisga'a Final Agreement: A treaty with the governments of BC and Canada that recognizes Nisga'a self-government and covers subjects such as land, water, forests, fisheries, wildlife and migratory birds, and environmental assessment and protection.

not-for-profit: An organization that provides a service or product that benefits a community. This type of business does not earn profits for its owners.

Order of Canada: An award given to citizens who have made an extraordinary contribution to the country.

origami: A craft using folded paper to make different designs.

origins: Beginnings.

Pacific Cooperative Union: Created to help farmers process and sell their fruit. Many of its members were of Japanese descent.

patented: Obtaining the legal right to create, manufacture, and sell an invention. A patent also prevents others from making and selling the item for a certain number of years.

Pearl Harbor: A naval base in Honolulu, Hawaii. On Sunday, December 7, 1941, the base was attacked by Japan. This led to the United States entering the Second World War.

performative masks: Masks used for performance during ceremonies.

period: A length of time; a distinct portion of history.

philanthropist: Someone who donates money or their skills to help others.

philosophy: Viewpoints – how people understand the world they live in.

polio: A disease that could make a person paralyzed or even die. It was very dangerous in children. Now we have a vaccine for it.

pre-emptions: The right given to settlers by the government to occupy tracts of land.

prefabricated: A building made in a factory and placed on a lot.

prism: A 3D object with triangular ends and rectangular sides. It is made from a transparent material like glass.

privileges: The rights or advantages a person or group of people have.

proverb: A short saying that offers a piece of advice or contains some wisdom.

punched card system: A piece of stiff paper holding numbers represented by the presence of holes in certain positions.

quests: Difficult searches for something of meaning.

racial discrimination: When a person is treated badly because of their skin colour, race, or where their family comes from.

racism: Prejudice against a racial group; a belief that people of races different from your own are not as good as you are.

racist: Someone who practises racism.

radiating: Spreading from a central point.

raptors: Birds that eat small mammals.

reciprocal: To give in return.

reciting: Reading aloud or repeating something you have memorized to an audience.

reclining: Lying down.

reference library: A library that focuses on documents with facts and information.

regalia: Clothing and objects used during ceremonial dances.

remanifesting: Returning from the spirit world to the physical world.

repatriation/repatriated: To return to the community it originally belonged to.

replica: An object that is created to look like the original.

representation: An accurate description of someone or something.

resources: Usually materials that people value and need.

rituals: Ceremonies made up of certain steps that happen in a certain order.

rooming house: A house with many bedrooms that are rented out. Renters share a bathroom and kitchen.

scribe: A person who copies a text or who writes down words dictated to them.

sedentary: Spending a lot of time seated; not getting much exercise.

seismic upgrade: The renovation or reconstruction of a building so it will be safer in a large earthquake.

semi-autobiographical: Based on the writer's own life but also has parts that are made up.

settlers: People who move to a new place with the idea of staying there.

simulate: A way to imitate something without actually having to do it.

smelting: Getting metal from its ore.

Soviet Union: Made up of 15 states, the Soviet Union was the first country to have a communist government. By December 1991, it was no longer a country and was replaced by 15 independent countries, including Russia, Ukraine, and Armenia.

spiritual: A feeling that connects to a person's soul.

superstructure: The raised deck of a ship.

sustainability/sustainably: Using natural resources in a way that isn't selfish without hurting the needs of future generations; with the environment in mind.

sustenance: Food or nourishment.

tangrams: A Chinese geometric puzzle.

temporary exhibits: Exhibits that will be in the museum for a limited time.

therapeutic: Treatment that makes a person better.

time immemorial: Going so far back in the past it's before memory and record.

tributaries: Rivers and streams that run into larger bodies of water like rivers and lakes.

unceded territory: Land that was never legally given up.

uranium: A shiny, white metal that is dangerous because it is radioactive. It can be used to make nuclear weapons.

visual language: Forms and shapes an artist uses.

War Measures Act: A law that gave the Canadian government extra power because the country was at war. The government controlled what was reported in the news and could hold people in prison or make them leave the country without a reason. It also controlled transportation, trade, and had the right to take people's belongings.

watershed: An area of land where all the water underneath it drains into a river or lake.

SELECTED SOURCES

WHAT CAN WE LEARN FROM THE PAST?

Chao-Fong, Léonie. "10 Facts about the Deadly 1918 Spanish Flu Epidemic." History Hit. https://www.historyhit.com/facts-about-the-deadly-1918-flu-epidemic/.

"Spit Spreads Death: The Influenza Pandemic of 1918–19 in Philadelphia." Mütter Museum. https://muttermuseum.org/exhibitions/spit-spreads-death.

BULKLEY VALLEY MUSEUM

Joseph Coyle's Egg Carton

Bulkley Valley Museum. "Joseph Coyle." Ingenium Channel. https://ingeniumcanada.org/channel/innovation/joseph-coyle.

"Joseph Coyle Invents the Egg Carton, 1911." Inventive Kids. https://inventivekids.com/joseph-coyle-invents-egg-carton-1911/.

Smith, M. Gale. "The Egg Carton Invented in BC." BC Food History. https://www.bcfoodhistory.ca/the-egg-carton-invented-in-bc/.

Tailor's Scissors

Bulkley Valley Museum. Aida Family Fonds. https://search.bvmuseum.org/list?q=Aida+family+fonds&p=1&ps=20.

KSAN HISTORICAL VILLAGE AND MUSEUM

"Meet the Gitxsan: They've Been Around for 10 Times Longer Than Canada." Daily Hive. https://dailyhive.com/vancouver/british-columbia-aboriginals-gitxsan.

haxsgwiikws (Whistle)

Rescan. *KSM Project: Gitxsan Nation Traditional Knowledge and Use Desk-Based Research Report*. Prepared for Seabridge Gold Inc. by Rescan Environmental Services Ltd., Vancouver, British Columbia. https://acee-ceaa.gc.ca/050/documents_staticpost/49262/89282/Chapter_30_Appendices/Appendix_30-D_Gitxsan_Tradnl_Use_Desk_Based_Research_Report.pdf.

hoobixim hasgaltxw matx (Goat Horn Spoon)

"Feeding the Ancestors: Tlingit Carved Horn Spoons." Past Exhibitions, Peabody Museum of Archaeology & Ethnology. https://peabody.harvard.edu/past-exhibitions.

"History of Northwest Coast Goat-Horn Spoons." Sealaska Heritage Institute. YouTube. https://www.youtube.com/watch?v=XhsGvgE-emo.

Kuhnlein, Harriet V., and Murray M. Humphries. "Traditional Animal Foods of Indigenous Peoples of Northern North America: The Contributions of Wildlife Diversity to the Subsistence and Nutrition of Indigenous Cultures." Centre for Indigenous Peoples' Nutrition and Environment, McGill University. http://traditionalanimalfoods.org/mammals/hoofed/page.aspx?id=6361.

Schwarcz, Joe. "What Is an 'Oolichan'?" Office for Science and Society, McGill University. https://www.mcgill.ca/oss/article/you-asked/what-oolichan.

Wilp Lax Gibuu (Wolf House)

Baker, Rafferty. "How Indigenous Culture Is Dancing Its Way into the Next Generation." *CBC News*. https://www.cbc.ca/news/canada/british-columbia/how-indigenous-culture-is-dancing-its-way-into-the-next-generation-1.4556682.

Rescan. *KSM Project: Gitxsan Nation Traditional Knowledge and Use Desk-Based Research Report*. Prepared for Seabridge Gold Inc. by Rescan Environmental Services Ltd., Vancouver, British Columbia. https://acee-ceaa.gc.ca/050/documents_staticpost/49262/89282/Chapter_30_Appendices/Appendix_30-D_Gitxsan_Tradnl_Use_Desk_Based_Research_Report.pdf.

KITIMAT MUSEUM & ARCHIVES

'íksduqʷia (Eagle) Frontlet

Laurence, Robin. "Lyle Wilson's Paint Is an Outstanding Cultural Experience." *The Georgia Straight*. https://www.straight.com/arts/370131/lyle-wilsons-paint-outstanding-cultural-experience.

"Wilson, Lyle." ABC BookWorld. https://abcbookworld.com/writer/wilson-lyle/.

Wilson, Lyle, Karen Duffek, Gary Wyatt, and Barbara Jean Duncan. *Paint: The Painted Works of Lyle Wilson*. Maple Ridge, BC: Maple Ridge Pitt Meadows Arts Council, 2012.

Kenney Dam Souvenir Pin

"Aluminum Facts." Government of Canada. https://www.nrcan.gc.ca/our-natural-resources/minerals-mining/minerals-metals-facts/aluminum-facts/20510.

"New Day Agreement." Cheslatta Carrier Nation. https://www.cheslatta.com/the-nation.

"Settlement and Reconciliation with the Cheslatta Carrier Nation." govTogetherBC. https://engage.gov.bc.ca/govtogetherbc/consultation/cheslatta/.

Smith, Charlie. "Broadcaster and Writer Ben Meisner Left a Mark with His Opposition to the Kemano Completion Project." *The Georgia Strait*. https://www.straight.com/news/424721/broadcaster-and-writer-ben-meisner-left-mark-his-opposition-kemano-completion-project.

Yellow Cedar x̄á'isla Family Pole

Barbetti, Louise, ed. *Haisla! We Are Our History: Our Lands, Nuyem and Stories as Told by Our Chiefs and Elders*. Kitamaat, BC: Kitamaat Village Council, 2005. https://docs2.cer-rec.gc.ca/ll-eng/llisapi.dll/fetch/2000/90464/90552/384192/620327/624910/693017/774474/D80-22-06_-_Haisla_Nation_-_5_Haisla-We_Are_Our_History_2005_Part1_-_A2K0V0.pdf?nodeid=774677&vernum=-2.

Griffith, Jane. "One Little, Two Little, Three Canadians: The Indians of Canada Pavilion and Public Pedagogy, Expo 1967." *Journal of Canadian Studies/Revue d'études canadiennes* 49, no. 2 (Spring 2015): 171–204. muse.jhu.edu/article/614385.

"Sammy Robinson." BC Achievement Foundation. https://www.bcachievement.com/awardee/sammy-robinson/.

Rutherdale Myra, and Jim Miller. "'It's Our Country': First Nations' Participation in the Indian Pavilion at Expo 67." *Journal of the Canadian Historical Association/Revue de la Société historique du Canada* 17, no. 2 (2006): 148–173. https://www.erudit.org/fr/revues/jcha/2006-v17-n2-jcha1833/016594ar.pdf.

HLI G̲OOTHL WILP-ADOK̲SHL NISG̲A'A (NISG̲A'A MUSEUM)
Mask of Gwaax̱ts'agat

Le Moigne, Yannick, Glyn Williams-Jones, Kelly Russell, and Steve Quane. "Physical Volcanology of Tseax Volcano, British Columbia, Canada." *Journal of Maps* 16, no. 2 (2020): 363–375. Taylor and Francis Online. https://www.tandfonline.com/doi/full/10.1080/17445647.2020.1758809.

Williams-Jones, Glyn, René W. Barendregt, James K. Russell, Yannick Le Moigne, Randolph J. Enkin, and Rose Gallo. "The Age of the Tseax Volcanic Eruption, British Columbia, Canada." *Canadian Journal of Earth Sciences* 57, no. 10 (October 2020). Canadian Science Publishing. https://cdnsciencepub.com/doi/10.1139/cjes-2019-0240.

SUNSHINE COAST MUSEUM & ARCHIVES
Charlotte Gibson's Lamp

Belongia, Edward A., and Allison L. Naleway. "Smallpox Vaccine: The Good, the Bad, and the Ugly." *Clinical Medicine & Research* 1, no. 2 (April 2003): 87–92. https://www.ncbi.nlm.nih.gov/pmc/articles/PMC1069029/.

"History of Smallpox." Centers for Disease Control and Prevention. https://www.cdc.gov/smallpox/history/history.html.

Jade Monkey

Blakemore, Erin. "How Mahatma Gandhi Changed Political Protest." *National Geographic.* https://www.nationalgeographic.com/culture/article/mahatma-gandhi-changed-political-protest.

"Gandhi's Three Monkeys by Subodh Gupta." Qatar Museums. https://qm.org.qa/en/visit/public-art/subodh-gupta-gandhis-three-monkeys/.

"Salt March." Britannica Kids. https://kids.britannica.com/students/article/Salt-March/624729.

"Teaching Tuesday: Three Wise Monkeys." Japan Information & Culture Center, Embassy of Japan, Washington, DC. https://www.us.emb-japan.go.jp/jicc/doc/Teaching%20Tuesday/2017/20170516threemonkeys.pdf.

"Three Wise Monkeys." Wikipedia. https://en.wikipedia.org/wiki/Three_wise_monkeys.

"Well-Known Expressions: See No Evil, Hear No Evil, Speak No Evil." BookBrowse. https://www.bookbrowse.com/expressions/detail/index.cfm/expression_number/671/see-no-evil-hear-no-evil-speak-no-evil.

QATHET MUSEUM & ARCHIVES

Rodmay Heritage Hotel French Fry Cutter

Percy, Sean. "Blast from the Past – Ghost Stories." *qathet Living.* https://issuu.com/powellriverliving/docs/2110_october_2021/s/13522527.

"The Rodmay Hotel." Townsite Heritage Society. http://www.tourism-powellriver.ca/blog/rodmay-hotel.

MUSEUM OF VANCOUVER

Douglas Fir (*Pseudotsuga menziesii*)

"Douglas-Fir." SQ'ÉWLETS. http://digitalsqewlets.ca/sqwelqwel/belongings-possessions/harvesting-recolte/fir_sapin-eng.php.

"Douglas-fir and the Mice." Nature Kids, BC. https://naturekidsbc.ca/douglas-fir-and-the-mice.

"Douglas-fir (*Pseudotsuga menziesii*)." University of California Agriculture and Natural Resources. https://ucanr.edu/sites/forestry/California_forests/http___ucanrorg_sites_forestry_California_forests_Tree_Identification_/Douglas-fir/.

"Douglas Fir *Pseudotsuga menziesii* (Pinaceae)." Shoreline Community College. https://library. shoreline.edu/treecampus/douglas_fir.

First City Seal of Vancouver

MacDonald, Norbert. "The Canadian Pacific Railway and Vancouver's Development to 1900." *BC Studies*, no. 35 (Autumn 1977). https://ojs.library.ubc.ca/index.php/bcstudies/ article/view/936.

Mackie, John. "This Week in History: Vancouver's Original Coat-of-Arms Turns Up on a City Ad for 'scavengering.'" *Vancouver Sun*. https://vancouversun.com/life/this-week-in- history-vancouvers-original-coat-of-arms-turns-up-on-a-city-ad-for-scavengering- vancouvers-original-coat-of-arms-turned-up-on-a-city-ad-for-scavengering.

"Symbols of the City of Vancouver." City of Vancouver. https://vancouver.ca/news-calendar/ city-symbols.aspx.

Shinto Household Shrine

"Celebrating Life in a Shinto Shrine." CBC Radio, *Tapestry*. https://www.cbc.ca/radio/ tapestry/a-spark-of-spirit-in-everything-1.3462036/celebrating-life-in-a-shinto- shrine-1.3462766.

Donaldson, Jesse. "There's a 'Lost' Japanese Village Hidden in North Vancouver's Watershed." *Montecristo Magazine*. https://montecristomagazine.com/highlights/ japanese-village-north-vancouver.

Greenberg, Mike. "Ebisu: The Japanese Lucky God." Mythology Source. https:// mythologysource.com/ebisu-japanese-god/.

"Shinto: A Japanese Religion." Asia Society. https://asiasociety.org/education/shinto.

Kitsilano Cougar Pelt

"Cougar in British Columbia." Government of British Columbia, Ministry of Environment, Environmental Stewardship Division. http://wwwt.env.gov.bc.ca/wld/documents/ cougar.htm.

"Cougars!" CRD. https://www.crd.bc.ca/docs/default-source/parks- pdf/2019cougarseducatorsguide.pdf?sfvrsn=159e82ca_2.

Gross, Liza. "Master Regulators: How Mountain Lions Boost Biodiversity." *PBS Nature*. https:// www.pbs.org/wnet/nature/blog/master-regulators-how-mountain-lions-boost- biodiversity/.

"Mammal with the Most Names." *Guinness World Records*. https://www.guinnessworldrecords. com/world-records/78143-mammal-with-the-most-names.

"Our Work: Science & Conservation." The Cougar Fund. https://www.cougarfund.org/science/.

Wáx̱ayus, Welcoming Salmon

"Ceremonies and Feasts in the Squamish and Líl'wat Nations." Squamish Líl'wat Cultural Centre. https://slcc.ca/ceremonies-and-feasts-in-the-squamish-and-lilwat-nations.

"History of the Sen̓áx̱w Lands." Sen̓áx̱w. https://senakw.com/history.

Laboucan, Amei-Lee. "A Century after Their Village Was Burned, Sḵwx̱wú7mesh Is Rebuilding Sen̓áx̱w." IndigiNews. https://indiginews.com/vancouver/a-century-after-their-village-was-destroyed-squamish-is-rebuilding-senakw.

"Mapping Tool: Kitsilano Reserve." indigenousfoundations.arts.ubc.ca. https://indigenousfoundations.arts.ubc.ca/mapping_tool_kitsilano_reserve/.

"Storytelling of the Origin of the Salmon People: S7a7ú7 ya tl'ik Sts'úkwi7 Stélmexw." YouTube. https://www.youtube.com/watch?v=WMsE1tD99mM.

MUSEUM OF ANTHROPOLOGY AT UBC

"About MOA." University of British Columbia. https://moa.ubc.ca/about-moa/.

Aird, Louise. "Dream Team: Architect Arthur Erickson & Landscape Architect Cornelia Hahn Oberlander." Louise Aird. https://www.louiseaird.com/blog/2013/07/03/dream-team-architect-arthur-erickson-landscape-architect-cornelia-hahn-oberlander.

Cherry, Alissa, and Katie Ferrante. "A Look Back to the Beginning: Seventy Years of MOA in the Making." University of British Columbia. https://moa.ubc.ca/2019/12/a-look-back-to-the-beginning-seventy-years-of-moa-in-the-making/.

"Great Hall Seismic Upgrades + Renewal." University of British Columbia. https://moa.ubc.ca/2020/12/great-hall-seismic-upgrades/.

Ten: A Musqueam Hanging

Morell, Virginia. "The Dogs That Grew Wool and the People Who Love Them." *Hakai Magazine*. https://hakaimagazine.com/features/the-dogs-that-grew-wool-and-the-people-who-love-them/.

The Raven and the First Men

"In Memoriam: Bill Reid (1920–1998)." Canadian Museum of History/Musée canadien de l'histoire. https://www.historymuseum.ca/cmc/exhibitions/aborig/reid/reid04e.html.

McMaster, Gerald. "Iljuwas Bill Reid: Life & Work." Art Canada Institute/L'Institut de l'art canadien. https://www.aci-iac.ca/art-books/iljuwas-bill-reid/biography/.

"Point Grey Battery." Fortwiki. http://www.fortwiki.com/Point_Grey_Battery.

"*The Raven and the First Men*." Museum of Anthropology, University of British Columbia. http://collection-online.moa.ubc.ca/search/item?keywords=The+Raven+and+First+men&row=5&tab=more.

"*The Raven and the First Men*: From Conception to Completion." Museum of Anthropology, University of British Columbia. https://moa.ubc.ca/2020/01/the-raven-and-the-first-men-from-conception-to-completion/.

Sheenan, Carol. "Bill Reid." The Canadian Encyclopedia. https://www.thecanadianencyclopedia.ca/en/article/william-ronald-reid.

"Who Was Bill Reid?" Bill Reid Gallery of Northwest Coast Art. https://www.billreidgallery.ca/pages/about-bill-reid.

Nininigamł (Earthquake Mask)

"Dzawada'enuxw of Kingcome Inlet." Dzawadaʼenuxw First Nation. https://www.kingcome.ca/people.

Finkbeiner, Ann. "The Great Quake and the Great Drowning." *Hakai Magazine*. https://hakaimagazine.com/features/great-quake-and-great-drowning/.

Giffard, Petra. "Shake Up: An Exhibition to Mark Seismic Upgrades at MOA." *The Source* 19, no. 11 (December 11, 2018–January 8, 2019). https://thelasource.com/en/2018/12/10/shake-up-an-exhibition-to-mark-seismic-upgrades-at-moa/.

Hanson, Erin. "Oral Traditions." indigenousfoundations.arts.ubc.ca. https://indigenousfoundations.arts.ubc.ca/oral_traditions/.

"Indigenous Knowledge + Earthquakes." Museum of Anthropology, University of British Columbia. https://moa.ubc.ca/wp-content/uploads/2020/11/IK-Earthquakes-FINAL.pdf.

Kramer, Jennifer. "Dancing Ninini: Learning about Earthquakes through Culture." Museum of Anthropology, University of British Columbia. https://moa.ubc.ca/2021/04/dancing-ninini-learning-about-earthquakes-through-culture/.

McMillan, Alan D., and Ian Hutchinson. "When the Mountain Dwarfs Danced: Aboriginal Traditions of Paleoseismic Events along the Cascadia Subduction Zone of Western North America." *Ethnohistory* 49, no. 1 (December 2002). https://www.researchgate.net/publication/31086309_When_the_Mountain_Dwarfs_Danced_Aboriginal_Traditions_of_Paleoseismic_Events_along_the_Cascadia_Subduction_Zone_of_Western_North_America.

Schulz, Kathryn. "The Really Big One." *The New Yorker*. https://www.newyorker.com/magazine/2015/07/20/the-really-big-one.

"Seismic Zones in Western Canada." Government of Canada. https://earthquakescanada.nrcan.gc.ca/zones/westcan-en.php.

K'lcta (Sea Monster Mask)

"Shake Up: Preserving What We Value." Museum of Anthropology, University of British Columbia. https://moa.ubc.ca/exhibition/shake-up/.

qeqən (Musqueam House Posts)

"House Post." Museum of Anthropology, University of British Columbia. http://collection-online.moa.ubc.ca/search/item?keywords=Susan+Point&row=36&tab=more.

Musqueam Indian Band. *Musqueam: A Living Culture*. Victoria, BC: CopperMoon Communications, 2006. https://juliegordon.com/uploads/Musqueam_LivingCulture_FINALPROOF.pdf.

Wilson, Jordan. "qeqən House Posts." *The Ubyssey*. YouTube. https://www.youtube.com/watch?v=1Hpa9kma8Fk.

'nik suugid 'wiileeksm waap (House-Front Board)

"Hematite Facts for Kids." Kiddle. https://kids.kiddle.co/Hematite.

"Minerals for Kids." Earth Sciences Museum, University of Waterloo. https://uwaterloo.ca/earth-sciences-museum/resources/just-kids/minerals-kids#Magnetite.

"Western Red Cedar, *Thuja plicata*." Native Plants PNW. http://nativeplantspnw.com/western-red-cedar-thuja-plicata/.

Leaf with Text from the Quran

Khatib, Ammar, and Nazir Khan. "The Origins of the Variant Readings of the Qur'an." Yaqeen Institute. https://yaqeeninstitute.ca/read/paper/the-origins-of-the-variant-readings-of-the-quran.

King Saud University. http://quran.ksu.edu.sa/translations/english/576.html.

"Kūfic Script." *Encyclopedia Britannica*. https://www.britannica.com/topic/Kufic-script.

"The Most Memorised Book on Earth – Part 3: My Quran Story." One Path Network. YouTube. https://www.youtube.com/watch?v=zPFxF7hRcHI.

"Qur'an Leaf in Kufic Script." Islamic Manuscripts. http://www.islamicmanuscripts.info/reference/books/Fraser-2006-Kwiatkowski/Fraser-2006-Kwiatkowski-040-061.pdf.

Tan, Enis Timuçin. "A Study of Kufic Script in Islamic Calligraphy and Its Relevance to Turkish Graphic Art Using Latin Fonts in the Late Twentieth Century." University of Wollongong, Australia. Academia. https://www.academia.edu/23460309/A_study_of_Kufic_script_in_Islamic_calligraphy_and_its_relevance_to_Turkish_graphic_art_using_Latin_fonts_in_the_late_twentieth_century.

Ghost Net Sea Creatures

Allam, Lorena. "Indigenous Cultural Views of the Shark." ABC Listen. https://www.abc.net.au/radionational/programs/earshot/indigenous-cultural-views-of-the-shark/6798174.

"Ghost Nets from the Ocean: Erub Arts Collaborative." Art Gallery of South Australia. https://agsa-prod.s3.amazonaws.com/media/dd/files/EDU_Resource_TARNANTHI17_ERUB.197654c.pdf.

Hernandez, Jon. "'Ghost Nets': How Lost and Abandoned Fishing Gear Is Destroying Marine Wildlife." *CBC News*. https://www.cbc.ca/news/canada/british-columbia/ghost-nets-lost-abandoned-fishing-gear-destroying-fish-stocks-marine-wildlife-1.5207474.

Mayer, Carol E. "T-Shirts + Turtles: Journeys to the Island of Erub." Museum of Anthropology, University of British Columbia. https://moa.ubc.ca/2020/06/t-shirts-turtles-journeys-to-the-island-of-erub/.

"NAIDOC Week: How First Nations People Are Saving Endangered Turtles." Great Barrier Reef Foundation. https://www.barrierreef.org/news/blog/naidoc-week-how-first-nations-people-are-saving-endangered-turtles.

"Torres Strait Island Stories and Messages Connecting Culture, the Ocean and Conservation." Erub Arts. http://www.erubarts.com.au/wp-content/uploads/2018/10/erub-stories-messages-2018-web.pdf.

HISTORIC JOY KOGAWA HOUSE

Joy's Desk

"Japanese Canadian Internment Sites of the Second World War (1942–49)." Government of British Columbia. https://www2.gov.bc.ca/assets/gov/driving-and-transportation/driving/japanese-internment-signs/slocan_extension_japanese_internment_camp.pdf.

SCIENCE WORLD

Davis, Chuck. "A Year in Five Minutes: Vancouver 1982." Spacing Vancouver. http://spacing.ca/vancouver/2010/12/30/a-year-in-five-minutes-vancouver-1982/.

"The Fascinating History behind the Iconic Science World (Photos)." 604 NOW. https://604now.com/science-world-vancouver-history/.

Scintillating Grid Illusion

Gregory, Richard L. "Knowledge in Perception and Illusion." *Philosophical Transactions of the Royal Society B* 352 (1997): 1121–1128. http://www.richardgregory.org/papers/knowl_illusion/knowledge-in-perception.pdf.

"Illusions." National Institute of Environmental Health Sciences. https://kids.niehs.nih.gov/games/riddles/illusions/index.htm.

"Optical Illusion Facts for Kids." Kiddle. https://kids.kiddle.co/Optical_illusion.

"What Is an Optical Illusion?" Optics 4 Kids. https://www.optics4kids.org/optical-illusions.

Stan the Dinosaur

Black, Riley. "A *T. Rex* Sold for $31.8 Million, and Paleontologists Are Worried." *Smithsonian Magazine.* https://www.smithsonianmag.com/science-nature/t-rex-sold-318-million-and-paleontologists-are-worried-180976071/.

"Facts about Stan the *T-rex*." Kenosha Public Museums. YouTube. https://www.youtube.com/watch?v=QaTSZQXvTQQ.

"Stan (dinosaur)." Wikipedia. https://en.wikipedia.org/wiki/Stan_(dinosaur).

Beaver Lodge

"The Beaver: Architect of Biodiversity." Ontario Parks. https://www.ontarioparks.com/parksblog/the-beaver-architect-of-biodiversity/.

MISSION MUSEUM

Bunjiro Sakon's Trunk

Bailey, Patricia G., and Donald J.C. Phillipson. "David Suzuki." The Canadian Encyclopedia. https://www.thecanadianencyclopedia.ca/en/article/david-suzuki.

Eldridge, Alison. "David Suzuki: Canadian Scientist, Television Personality, Author, and Activist." Britannica. https://www.britannica.com/biography/David-Suzuki.

Samsudin, Syafiqah. "Childhood." David Suzuki. https://blogs.ntu.edu.sg/hp3203-2017-21/about-david-suzuki/influences-in-childhood/.

Netting Needle

"History of Gifting." Joi Gifts. https://www.joigifts.com/blog/history-traditions-gifting-around-world/.

Wallin, Lisa. "The Story Behind the Japanese Custom of Shichi-Go-San (Seven-Five-Three)." *Tokyo Weekender*. https://www.tokyoweekender.com/2017/10/the-story-behind-the-japanese-custom-of-shichi-go-san-seven-five-three/.

BRITANNIA SHIPYARDS NATIONAL HISTORIC SITE

Murakami House Ofuroba (Bathing Room)

"A Brief History of Japanese Canadians in Manitoba." Japanese Cultural Association of Manitoba Inc. https://www.jcamwpg.ca/japanese-canadians-in-manitoba/.

Lazarus, Eve. "Asayo Murakami." Eve Lazarus. https://evelazarus.com/tag/asayo-murakami/.

Chinese Bunkhouse

Chan, Anthony B. "Chinese Canadians." The Canadian Encyclopedia. https://www.thecanadianencyclopedia.ca/en/article/chinese-canadians.

"Q&A with the Rt. Hon. Adrienne Clarkson." Innovating Canada. https://www.innovatingcanada.ca/diversity/supporting-newcomers-refugees/qa-with-the-rt-hon-adrienne-clarkson/.

MUSEUM OF SURREY

"The History of Surrey's Museum and Archives." Surrey History. https://www.surreyhistory.ca/museumarchives.html.

Semiahmoo Petroglyph

Blakemore, Erin. "Radiocarbon Helps Date Ancient Objects – But It's Not Perfect." *National Geographic*. https://www.nationalgeographic.com/culture/article/radiocarbon-dating-explained.

"Carbon Dating." Mocomi.com. https://mocomi.com/carbon-dating/.

"Carbon Facts." Mocomi.com. https://mocomi.com/carbon-facts/.

"Elements for Kids: Carbon." Ducksters. https://www.ducksters.com/science/chemistry/carbon.php.

Jacquard Loom

"Brocade." Britannica. https://www.britannica.com/technology/brocade.

Charkes, Ella. "2,000 Years of Elegance: The Story of Damask." Schumacher. https://fschumacher.com/blog/history-of-damask/.

"Programming Patterns: The Story of the Jacquard Loom." Science + Industry Museum. https://www.scienceandindustrymuseum.org.uk/objects-and-stories/jacquard-loom.

Freda Gunst's Buggy

Wylie, Leslie. "Olympic Girl Power: The Incredible Story of Lis Hartel." Horse Nation: Horsing Around the World. https://www.horsenation.com/2014/11/17/olympic-girl-power-the-incredible-story-of-lis-hartel/.

Berry Basket from Ota Family Farm

"Acadia." Britannica Kids. https://kids.britannica.com/kids/article/Acadia/443550.

"Expulsion of the Acadians Facts for Kids." Kiddle. https://kids.kiddle.co/Expulsion_of_the_ Acadians.

"Golden Miles of History: The Minto Japanese Canadian World War II Internment Camp Site." Lillooet Guaranteed Rugged. https://lillooet.ca/Recreation-Activities/Golden-Miles-of-History/Japanese-Canadians-in-Lillooet/The-Minto-Japanese-Canadian-World-War-II-Interment.aspx.

"Minto Mine." Canada's Historic Places. https://www.historicplaces.ca/en/rep-reg/place-lieu.aspx?id=23077.

_K de K_ Ferry Wheel

"Brownsville." Surrey History. https://www.surreyhistory.ca/brownsville.html.

Harris, Ashley. "The 'Longest Free Ferry in the World' Is in BC & Its Views Are Absolutely Stunning (Photos)." Narcity. https://www.narcity.com/longest-free-ferry-in-the-world-is-in-bc-views-are-stunning.

True Surrey. "The Importance of One Little Ferry." Discover Surrey. https://discoversurreybc.com/blog/historic-bridgeview.

FRASER RIVER DISCOVERY CENTRE

Fin Donnelly's Fraser River Swim Gear

Branco, Dave. "26 Years Later, Fin Donnelly Remembers Swimming the Length of the Fraser River." CKPG Today. https://ckpgtoday.ca/2021/06/09/26-years-later-fin-donnelly-remembers-swimming-the-length-of-the-fraser-river/.

Colebourn, John. "Man Who Swam Fraser River Now Guides Young Adults on Famed Waterway." _Times Colonist_. https://www.timescolonist.com/news/b-c/man-who-swam-fraser-river-now-guides-young-adults-on-famed-waterway-1.1266523.

Smith, Charlie. "Fin Donnelly and Rivershed Society of BC Prime Next Generation to Fight for the Fraser River." _The Georgia Straight_. https://www.straight.com/news/755556/fin-donnelly-and-rivershed-society-bc-prime-next-generation-fight-fraser-river.

Zillich, Tom. "Man Who Twice Swam the Length of BC's Longest River Named to Fraser River Hall of Fame." *Tofino-Ucluelet Westerly News*. https://www.westerlynews.ca/news/man-who-twice-swam-the-length-of-b-c-s-longest-river-named-to-fraser-river-hall-of-fame/.

George the White Sturgeon

"BC White Sturgeon: Life History, Lifecycle and Population Decline." Government of Canada. https://www.pac.dfo-mpo.gc.ca/education/lessonplans-lecons/sturgeon-esturgeon-eng.html.

Hatfield, Todd, Steve McAdam, and Troy Nelson. *Impacts to Abundance and Distribution of Fraser River White Sturgeon: A Summary of Existing Information and Presentation of Impact Hypotheses*. https://frasersturgeon.com/wp-content/uploads/2019/01/Fraser-Impact-hypothesis-2004.pdf.

Jackson, Sarah, Mackenzie Mercer, and Shane Steele. "Distribution and Migration of Acoustic-Transmitter Tagged White Sturgeon with Special Regards to Overwintering Habitat in the Lower Fraser River 2017–2018." British Columbia Institute of Technology, Fish, Wildlife, and Recreation Program. https://frasersturgeon.com/wp-content/uploads/2019/01/Sturgeon-Report-2017-2018.pdf.

"White Sturgeon." British Columbia Ministry of Environment, Lands and Parks. https://www2.gov.bc.ca/assets/gov/environment/plants-animals-and-ecosystems/species-ecosystems-at-risk/brochures/white_sturgeon.pdf.

"White Sturgeon: An Uncertain Future for the Dinosaur of Our Rivers." Keystone Environmental. https://keystoneenvironmental.ca/white-sturgeon-an-uncertain-future-for-the-dinosaur-of-our-rivers/.

ABOUT THE AUTHORS

S. Lesley Buxton is the author of the award-winning memoir, *One Strong Girl: Surviving the Unimaginable – A Mother's Memoir*. Her essays have appeared in *Hazlitt, Today's Parent, Still Standing, This Magazine,* and in the Caitlin Press anthology, *Love Me True*. An excerpt of *One Strong Girl* appeared in the March 2019 issue of *Reader's Digest* and has been translated into Spanish. For 18 years, she ran her own business, travelling around Ottawa and western Quebec teaching theatre and creative writing to children and teens. She has an MFA in creative nonfiction from the University of King's College in Halifax, Nova Scotia. To learn more about her, visit www.slesleybuxton.com.

Sue Harper is a retired secondary school teacher who has a BSc in psychology, an MA in English language and literature, and an MFA in creative nonfiction. She has co-authored ten textbooks for the Ontario secondary English curriculum and has written three books for reluctant readers as part of the series, The Ten, published by Scholastic. Her writing can also be found in magazines in Canada (*NUVO, Okanagan Life*), the United Kingdom (*France Magazine*), and New Zealand (*North and South Magazine, Forest and Bird*). In 2019, she published her memoir, *Winter in the City of Light: A Search for Self in Retirement*. She is the only person she knows who has explored all six hectares of Paris's Louvre Museum. To learn more, visit http://seniornomad.wordpress.com.

INDEX